D0842547

An Illustrated History of the Olympics

The 1984 Olympic Games: Sarajevo/Los Angeles

RFK

Turned On

Instant Replay (with Jerry Kramer)

Distant Replay (with Jerry Kramer)

Bo Knows Bo (with Bo Jackson)

Absolutely Mahvelous (with Billy Crystal)

.44 (with Jimmy Breslin)

Massacre at Winged Foot

The Masters

The Perfect Jump

Steinbrenner!

Joy in Mudville (with Mort Gerberg)

Simms to McConkey (with Phil Simms and Phil McConkey)

GAY OLYMPIAN

G A Y

by Tom Waddell

OLYMPIAN

The Life and Death of Dr. Tom Waddell

and Dick Schaap

 Alfred A. Knopf New York 1996

THIS IS A BORZOI BOOK
PUBLISHED BY ALFRED A. KNOPF, INC.

Copyright © 1996 by The Thomas F. Waddell Trust and Dick Schaap
All rights reserved under International and Pan-American Copyright Conventions.
Published in the United States by Alfred A. Knopf, Inc., New York,
and simultaneously in Canada by Random House of Canada Limited, Toronto.
Distributed by Random House, Inc., New York.

http://www.randomhouse.com/

Grateful acknowledgment is made to the following for permission to reprint
previously published material: *The Advocate*: Excerpt from profile of Tom Waddell
by Randy Shilts (*The Advocate*, July 1976). Reprinted courtesy of Liberation
Publications Inc. *The New York Times Company*: Excerpts from "Public & Private:
Game Time" by Anna Quindlen (*The New York Times*, 6/25/94), and from an
editorial "Invisible People Made Visible" (*The New York Times*, 6/28/94),
copyright © 1994 by The New York Times Company. Reprinted by permission of
The New York Times Company. *Random House, Inc.*: Excerpt from "Lullaby,"
from *Collected Poems* by W. H. Auden, copyright © 1940 and renewed 1968
by W. H. Auden. Reprinted by permission of Random House, Inc.
The Society of Authors: "To an Athlete Dying Young," Poem XIX from
A Shropshire Lad by A. E. Housman. Reprinted by permission of The Society
of Authors as the literary representative of the Estate of A. E. Housman.

Library of Congress Cataloging-in-Publication Data
Waddell, Tom, 1937–1987.
Gay Olympian: the life and death of Dr. Tom Waddell /
by Tom Waddell and Dick Schaap. — 1st ed.
p. cm.
ISBN 0-394-57223-8
1. Waddell, Tom, 1937–1987.
2. Gay athletes—United States—Biography.
3. Gay Games.
I. Schaap, Dick.
II. Title.
GV697.W33A3 1996
796'.092—dc20
[B]95-31223
CIP

Manufactured in the United States of America
First Edition

To the people with AIDS

who are fighting as bravely as Tom did

To an Athlete Dying Young

The time you won your town the race
We chaired you through the market-place;
Man and boy stood cheering by,
And home we brought you shoulder-high.

Today, the road all runners come,
Shoulder-high we bring you home,
And set you at your threshold down,
Townsman of a stiller town.

Smart lad, to slip betimes away
From fields where glory does not stay
And early though the laurel grows
It withers quicker than the rose.

Eyes the shady night has shut
Cannot see the record cut,
And silence sounds no worse than cheers
After earth has stopped the ears:

Now you will not swell the rout
Of lads that wore their honors out,
Runners whom renown outran
And the name died before the man.

So set, before its echoes fade,
The fleet foot on the sill of shade,
And hold to the low lintel up
The still-defended challenge-cup.

And round that early-laureled head
Will flock to gaze the strengthless dead,
And find unwithered on its curls
The garland briefer than a girl's.

—A. E. Housman

Foreword

Two weeks after Gay Games IV ended in New York in 1994, less than a month after I came out at the Games' opening ceremonies—"It's great to be out and proud," I said—I went to the U.S. Olympic Festival in St. Louis to accept the Robert J. Kane Award, named after the former president of the United States Olympic Committee.

The award is presented annually to "an American athlete who achieved success at the U.S. Olympic Festival, who continues to give back to his or her sport and who exemplifies the spirit and ideals of Bob Kane, including fairness, a commitment to excellence, and a dedication to sport and athletics."

"I accept the Robert J. Kane Award with humble gratitude," I told a thousand people at a breakfast in St. Louis, "and I'd like to dedicate it to the memory of Dr. Tom Waddell, an Olympic athlete who died of AIDS on July 11, 1987."

It was one thing for me to come out at the Gay Games. My words then were on videotape, and my audience at Columbia University's Wien Stadium was overwhelmingly gay and lesbian, overwhelmingly supportive. My words were greeted by tremendous applause.

But it was an entirely different thing to come out in person in front of a group of people, almost all of them straight, celebrating the U.S. Olympic Festival, many of them officials who had been shocked and offended by Tom Waddell's desire to call *his* festival the Gay Olympics. Some of those officials had been part of the campaign to strip the word "Olympics" from the title of the Gay Games, part of the campaign to harass and sue Tom Waddell.

I was terrified when I spoke in St. Louis, more frightened than if I had been called on to execute a demanding dive perfectly to win a gold medal. I was sweating. I was shaking. But I went on to pay tribute to Tom Waddell's skills and his spirit, his "fairness," his "commitment to excellence," his "dedication to sport and athletics." I pointed out that Tom had "founded the Gay Games, an Olympic-style event that embraces many of the same ideals that the Olympics and the Robert J. Kane Award are intended to celebrate." The applause at that point was less than thunderous.

Then I did something that I suspect Tom would have applauded. I urged the U.S. officials to do everything they could to prevent the 1996 Olympic volleyball preliminary matches from being held in Cobb County, Georgia, a community not far from Atlanta that had passed a resolution condemning "lifestyles advocated by the gay community."

Three weeks later, the Atlanta Organizing Committee announced that the volleyball matches would not be played in Cobb County. I was proud that I had stood up for my beliefs with a fraction of the courage Tom Waddell always displayed in standing up for his.

I never met Tom, even though our Olympic careers at least somewhat overlapped. In 1976, eight years after he competed in the decathlon in Mexico City, he was a member of the Saudi Arabian delegation to the Montreal Olympics, and I was a sixteen-year-old diver for the United States, eight years away from winning my first gold medal.

But still I feel that I knew Tom Waddell, that I shared many of his dreams and frustrations. We both loved dance and gymnastics long before we were Olympians; we both loved to perform. We both survived painful relationships with our fathers, and with lovers. Even though we both realized when we were young that we were attracted to men, we liked women and did not feel threatened by them. In fact, we both made love to women, both struggled with our sexual orientation and felt that we had to hide our homosexuality while competing in the Olympics.

I am grateful to Tom for creating the Gay Games, because it was through the Games that I was emboldened to come out, through the Games that I met the people who encouraged me to tell the story of my life.

Now I have read the story of Tom's life, and the proof that I have been moved and inspired is the simple fact of my having read the book from start to finish. That isn't easy for me. I am dyslexic, and reading can be a painful exercise.

Reading Tom's story was painful—I know what it's like to learn that you are HIV-positive, to face your own mortality—and at the same time immensely pleasurable.

I wish we could have been teammates. But, of course, in a sense we were.

Greg Louganis, 1996

GAY OLYMPIAN

Introduction

*We were flying to San Francisco in December 1986, the pro-
ducer and I, on our way to begin shooting a story for ABC-
TV's 20/20 on Tom Waddell, a former Olympic athlete who
was dying of AIDS. "I'm worried about this story," the producer said to me.*

"Why?" I said.

*"Because stories about homosexuals make me nervous," the
producer said, "and I think they make viewers nervous, too."*

*A few hours later the producer and I met Tom Waddell for
the first time, and spent the afternoon with him. Then the producer and I drove to our hotel.*

*The producer turned to me. "This is going to be a great
story," he said.*

"Why?" I said.

"Because I love this guy," Rob Wallace, the producer, said.

In the days when Tom Waddell lay dying of AIDS, a friend
asked Jessica, his daughter, who was about to be four, what she
would like to do when she grew up, and Jessica, who was very
blonde and very beautiful, widened her blue eyes and said,
"Everything."

She was, truly, Tom Waddell's daughter.

He did everything.

Tom lived not quite fifty years, but his life was an adventure that led him from Paterson, New Jersey, to Addis Ababa
and Odessa, to Bora Bora and Jidda, an adventure that filled
him with wonderment and excitement, with incredible pleasure and occasional pain.

Thirty-six hours before he died, Tom folded his hands on

his lap and said, as he had said so many times before, "Well, this should be interesting."

Then he slipped into a coma and never spoke coherently again.

Tom Waddell was an extraordinary human being. He was an artist—a painter, photographer, and dancer—and he was an athlete—a college football player, gymnast, and track-and-field star, so gifted, versatile, and dedicated that at the age of thirty he won a place on the 1968 United States Olympic team as a decathlete. In the Games in Mexico City, Tom finished sixth in the decathlon, an event that is often considered the ultimate test of athletic ability. He came in behind only one other American, the gold-medalist, Bill Toomey.

Tom was also a paratrooper in the United States Army and a physician. He specialized, ironically, in infectious diseases, and he was once ship's doctor on a Scripps Institution of Oceanography expedition to the South Pacific, and once personal physician to the brother of the king of Saudi Arabia.

"Many days, after I was long gone and tired," Bill Toomey said of the track-and-field tours he and Waddell shared in Africa and South America, "Tom would go to a local hospital and work all night on patients with tropical diseases."

Tom's acquaintances ranged from Adnan Khashoggi, the billionaire Saudi businessman—"Adnan," Waddell once said, flying aboard Khashoggi's private jet, "at the risk of offending you, I'd like to talk to you about your weight"—to Alan Cranston, the senator from California, a track-and-field buff who was the last person to talk to Tom on the telephone before he slipped into his final coma.

Tom Waddell, of course, was flawed, imperfect. He was sometimes stubborn, sometimes fickle, sometimes manipulative, and for a long time he was dangerously promiscuous. But he managed to combine, in dazzling doses, strength and sensitivity, intelligence and courage, compassion and combativeness. He contradicted all the stereotypes of the athlete—and of the homosexual.

In 1982 Tom conceived and nurtured the Gay Olympic Games, an athletic festival dedicated but not restricted to homosexuals, an event designed to foster both gay pride and the traditional Olympic ideal: "To educate people through sport in a spirit of better understanding."

The United States Olympic Committee demonstrated little or no understanding of Tom's idea. The USOC obtained an injunction depriving Tom of the use of the word "Olympic." (The committee has often taken legal action against establishments that have tried to utilize the name, even Greek restaurants.) He was ordered to call his competition simply the Gay Games, which distressed yet amused him.

"I say 'Gay Games' to a gay person," he once said, "and you know what kind of reaction I get? Just imagine! Drag races? Pocketbook races? Spoon-and-egg races? What do you mean, Gay Games?" Tom laughed. He could poke fun at his own sexuality, and at his own athletic ability.

When he won the gold medal for the javelin throw in Gay Games II in 1986, only a few weeks after learning that he had AIDS, acquired immune deficiency syndrome, he shrugged off his rather remarkable achievement. "It's a technique event," he said self-deprecatingly.

Tom devoted time and energy to the Gay Games in 1982, and again in 1986, when he knew that he was dying, because he believed passionately in the concept. Here was a chance to destroy homosexual stereotypes, a chance to dignify and motivate homosexual athletes, a chance to bridge the gap that had long existed between gay men and lesbian women.

He had always loved women—gay and straight—as friends and equals, and he was able to bridge the gap personally. When he met Sara Lewinstein, a professional bowler and a skilled softball and racquetball player who served with him on the committee that administered the Gay Games, he found in her someone who shared his zest for sports—and his dream of parenthood.

Sara and Tom had each been searching for someone with whom to have a child, someone they liked and respected and admired. They worked with each other throughout the Gay Games, saw each other respond to tension and to responsibility, and one day Sara asked Tom, "How would you like to have a baby with me?"

Tears came to Tom's eyes, and immediately he said yes and yes and yes. "I felt like I had proposed," Sara said.

At the end of the first Gay Games, long before Tom even suspected he had AIDS, he and Sara went away together and conceived a child. "How?" Tom was frequently asked. "The usual way," he said, smiling, tilting again at stereotypes. Jessica was born in August 1983. She was Tom's, and Sara's, greatest adventure.

Although Tom and Sara did not live together, they married, and Jessica Waddell Lewinstein—the order of her names, prompted by Sara, was Tom's small statement against sexism—divided her time between their two homes. Dianne Feinstein, then mayor of San Francisco, and The Grateful Dead, the rock group, were among the friends who contributed to the purchase of a handsome rocking horse that welcomed Jessica to the Bay Area.

"I can't come up with enough superlatives to tell you what it is like to be a daddy to this little girl who is just the most remarkable thing that's ever happened to me in my life," Tom told me soon after we met. Probably the happiest moment in his final year was when he learned that neither Sara nor Jessica carried any trace of the AIDS virus.

A few weeks before Tom died, Jessica helped him walk from his bed to the bathroom, helped him balance on withered athletic legs. She held his hand and guided him for a few painful steps. Some hours before he lost consciousness, Tom called Jessica to his bedside to say goodbye. He told her how much he loved her, how precious she was to him and to her mommy, and he handed his little girl a parting present—a small and sparkling crystal ball. "A wizard lived in this house before me," Tom told his child, "and he left behind this magic ball, which I am now giving to you."

He did leave magic, a special presence that a three-year-old could sense. "I know Daddy is dead," Jessica said at a gathering that celebrated Tom's life a few days after his death, "but I wish the angels could bring him back. I miss Daddy."

I miss her daddy, too.

I knew Tom Waddell for only seven months—and during that time he was always in pain and occasionally admitted it—but his impact was unmistakable. Some people instinctively sense other people's weaknesses and go for the jugular; Tom instinctively sensed the strengths of others and aimed for them. He had a rare genius for making people feel significant, valuable, special, better about themselves.

My wife, Trish, and I spent Tom's last conscious day sitting in his bedroom with him and two of his close friends, Eric Wilkinson and Suellen Manning. Trish had met Tom for the first time the previous day. His memory was betraying him, his ability to articulate fleeing. He spoke sparingly and softly, among friends who knew he was leaving them and were angry because they were losing him yet relieved because he was escaping from the pain. He comforted us.

"I know this sounds strange," Trish said when Tom finally slept, and we left his room, "but I had the most wonderful day."

I met Tom Waddell because I wanted to do a story about him for 20/20. When I won approval for the project (with surprising ease, encountering not a hint of homophobic resistance at ABC) and began to research the program, I called an official at the United States Olympic Committee—a friend of mine for thirty years—and asked him how I could get in touch with Bill Toomey to talk to him about a story I was doing about Tom Waddell.

"Why do you want to do a story about some fag and some dyke having a kid?" the USOC official said.

That was a classic manifestation of the diseases Tom Waddell battled all his brief life, the diseases of ignorance and prejudice. By comparison, AIDS was almost manageable.

"I've got AIDS," Tom told me the day I met him. "And I look at the statistics, I look at what that means, and I'm given a set of choices. I can freak out, which isn't going to do any good at all, or I can say this is what is."

He spoke calmly, rationally, soothingly. Deep into his illness he still looked like an athlete, six feet one, lean and sturdy.

"I've got approximately seven months between episodes of pneumocystis," he continued. "What am I going to do with that? Am I going to put my head under the sheets and just scream and yell and cry? No, I can't do that. I just don't want to take that route.

"I have my tears. I can lie here at night thinking, *Gee, Jessica's three years old. If I could only somehow be around when she's eighteen, and I could see her in her first chiffon dress.* And I cry. But that's good for me. I mean, that's good for anybody, to cry.

"Crying is a wonderful way to get rid of toxins, and then you have to say, *Okay, now let's get on with what I think is real.* And what is real is that there are still things to be said, things to be done, things that I can teach."

Tom Waddell maintained a journal for his daughter that he began before she was born. "My dear child," he wrote, "you must know some things about me to understand more about your own life, and how you came to be."

A Journal for Jessica

January 30, 1983

Soon I'll be welcoming you to this world. Sara and I decided we wanted to give you life.

We chose each other for this. Something was right concerning the timing, the feelings, the desire and the need. We felt right about each other and we both wanted to complete our lives in a way we had always believed would happen.

Before I met your mother, I had been wishing for you for years. But never did I imagine what my partner would be like—no one ever quite fit before.

Your mother, being an amazingly beautiful and determined woman, spoke first—and I seized upon her offer instantly. This took place during Gay Games I, and though the event—your conception—was put on the back burner till the Games were over, the thought of, the anticipation of, and the sharing with Sara of the secret plan have been such a joy and solace to me.

My expectations contain a great deal of fantasy when I think of *how* you will be in the phases of your growth. However, *what* you will be, in any sense, will be mostly up to you and I will not burden you with any expectations I may be harboring.

I will try to teach you many things, and I will attempt to make you a self-approving, self-sufficient, kind and understanding, concerned and wise person. Though it may sound arrogant and presumptuous of me to want these things, nevertheless I feel strongly that these are the most important gifts I can give you in preparation for a fulfilling lifetime.

These attributes will serve you well, and you must use them with humility because they degenerate without it!

Your mother will add other important and necessary elements to your character. She will show you humor and playfulness, courage and honor, and her own wisdom—which has a warm justice as its main component. These are her traits and if being exposed to them means you may acquire them, then you are fortunate indeed!

I am often asked what I wish your gender to be.

When your mother and I began planning, I assumed without having given it any thought that you would be a boy.

As we went on and the planning became serious, I began to question why I had that expectation.

I guess it was because that was my conditioning, as it is for most people. We live in a male-dominated culture and males are generally favored over females in most segments of that culture. It is, first of all, a mythical attitude, and, second, it is erroneous. If I teach you nothing else, dear child, please let it be the knowledge that you can think of yourself as a *person* first, and of your gender, class (we do live in a class structure) and heritage as simply the colors of your character.

It matters not to me what your gender will be. I want to do what I need to do during the period that you will imagine me omnipotent, along with your mother.

After that I would like us to be friends—that's above and beyond the mysterious attachment parent and child always carry for each other.

Tom Waddell *prayed* to be straight. When he was a child, an acolyte in the Catholic Church, he built an altar in his home and prayed each night to the icons that adorned it "for deliverance from this thing that was afflicting me that I couldn't talk to anybody about."

He knew from the age of six or seven that he was aroused by men, not women, excited by glimpses of his father naked, not his mother. He sometimes thought of challenging his instincts, of confronting them head-on, by becoming a priest.

But more often he thought of running his hands up a priest's frock.

"Frocks really used to turn me on," he recalled during the final year of his life. "But to this day, I've never had sex with a priest."

It was one of his few regrets, he admitted, but not a major one.

Tom Waddell *tried* to be straight. When he was a teenager he dated girls and labored at the art of petting. "I got some tit today," one of his friends once told him.

"Oh," said Tom. "What's it like?"

"It's great," the friend said.

The next time Tom called on a girl whose parents were out for the evening, he sat on the couch next to her and let his arm fall around her shoulders. "I figured if I could just get some tit," he explained, "I could get over this feeling I had."

But every time Tom's fingers inched toward the girl's breasts, she picked up his hand and lifted it away.

"I tried and I tried and I tried," Tom said, "but I never did get any tit. The idea seemed pretty ridiculous, anyway."

Neither praying nor petting helped.

"I thought I was the only homosexual in New Jersey," Tom Waddell said.

February 1, 1983

Tonight we had a nice dinner at Albion [Tom's handsome
sprawling home on Albion Street in the Mission district of
San Francisco], with Mom, Chris [Puccinelli, Sara's lover],
Zohn [Artman, Tom's lover], Bert and Renee Kael. Bert is a
pediatrician at Kaiser Hospital. Renee is a child psychologist.
You, my child, were the main topic of discussion.

Bert and Renee were puzzled by our plan to have and
raise you. While being extremely intelligent and liberal, they
had many questions that were indicative of a low consciousness of sexuality. They couldn't understand how two homosexual people could have children, because in their minds
sexuality was black and white.

They thought that a person is either one thing or another
with nothing in-between. Your Mom and I explained that
procreative desires and capacities may reside in everyone, in
spite of sexual orientation, that sexuality was a spectrum and
not a black-and-white situation.

How much we love you already!

P.S. Mom also related how we met and what her designs
were on me. I don't think she originally figured on allowing a
father to share fully in the process, but I made it very clear
very early that that was a necessity for me.

Paterson lies in the valley under the Passaic Falls . . .
the thunder of the waters filling his dreams . . .
—Paterson,
William Carlos Williams

Tom Waddell was born Thomas Joseph Michael Flubacher, the second of three children—all sons—of Elmer and
Marion Jardon Flubacher, both first-generation Americans

whose parents were born in Alsace-Lorraine. Marion Jardon's parents were French-speaking Alsatians, Elmer Flubacher's German-speaking. The families were not close.

Tom was born at 6:30 a.m. on November 1, 1937, in St. Joseph's Hospital in Paterson, New Jersey, a small industrial city less than twenty-five miles west of Manhattan. During the 1800s thousands of Germans, Italians, and Scandinavians settled in Paterson to work in its textile mills, particularly the silk factories. But the history of the "Silk City" went back to before the earliest days of European (Dutch) settlement.

"In a deep-set valley between hills almost hid by dense foliage lay the little village," William Carlos Williams wrote in his epic poem *Paterson*. "Dominated by the Falls the surrounding country was a beautiful wilderness where mountain pink and wood violet throve: a place inhabited only by straggling trappers and wandering Indians."

In *Paterson*, Williams alluded to two of the city's more notorious sons, a nineteenth-century daredevil named Sam Patch and a twentieth-century intellectual named Allen Ginsberg. To amuse himself, and others, Patch jumped off waterfalls. He conquered the Passaic Falls and the Niagara, but in 1829 he disappeared in the Genesee in upstate New York; a year later his body was found frozen in a cake of ice. Ginsberg preferred *literary* risks. He was, along with the novelist Jack Kerouac, one of the powerful voices of the Beat Generation, the composer of *Howl*, his epic poem. On occasion, Allen Ginsberg described himself as a homosexual communist Jewish poet.

Tom Waddell was not the only homosexual in New Jersey.

February 3, 1983

Your Mom has been very upset. There are rumors getting back to her from some women in her circle—women who are mostly in the bars and heavily ghettoized. They are very

threatened by what is happening, and they are basically insecure. Their rhetoric is of such meanness and so impoverished,
it is laughable.

Mom was accused of "having Tom Waddell's baby" so
that she could grab power in the community. Your Mom is a
very strong woman and she would like to get the ringleader
of the group that is spreading these stories in an alley and
beat the shit out of her.

But your Mom is also very wise. We talked at Artemis [a
restaurant owned by Sara, catering primarily to gay women],
and I told her how silly and funny it all is. I told her that she
should greet such remarks with humor. *That* is totally disarm-
ing! To react with anger only gives the low thinkers a button
to push—and then your Mom would suffer more.

I told her today that if she wanted your last name to be
Lewinstein, regardless of your gender, it would be fine with
me. She looked at me and smiled and said, "Yeah?"

I said, "Yeah!"

I really don't care what your name is. You will be *our*
child, and your name is of no consequence to me. It is more
important to Mom for lots of reasons that are easy to understand. She is a proud person—and also proud of her family
and heritage. It's important for family reasons, as well as preserving your Mom's sense of independence. You see, I really
like those things about her.

We talked a lot, and we felt very close to each other. Our
friendship becomes more trusting all the time, and I think
Mom is beginning to know how much I love her. I still feel her
keeping her distance in some important ways, but I will continue to try to erode any of her anxieties. I would like to become one of her *closest* friends.

I think of you often. I put my hand on Mom's belly
(when she permits it) to let you know that I am out here
waiting for you.

I'm afraid I envy Chris being able to kiss Mom's belly when they sleep together. Perhaps I'll put in a request.

Tom Flubacher spent his early years in poverty, he and his parents and his brothers trapped in Paterson's post-Depression working-class slums. When his father could not find work, the family was forced to live in a single crowded room in the home of Tom's sternly Germanic paternal grandparents. His grandfather was a firefighter in Haledon, New Jersey; his grandmother was in charge of sounding the town's noon-hour horn. "I never had the impression that they cared to have me around," Tom said.

Gradually the family's finances improved. Elmer Flubacher built airplane engines at the local Wright-Patterson plant. He also worked as a dyer in a textile mill. His wife was an office worker in the mill. They were able to move to an apartment behind an ice-cream parlor.

In none of his childhood homes, as far as he could remember, did Tom ever see a newspaper or a book, or ever hear a phonograph record or a discussion that went beyond the weather or the food on the table. Even more frustrating, he perceived no love, not between his parents, not from them for him or for his brothers. And his brothers themselves were strangers to Tom. Arthur, the older one, was uncommonly wild; Richard, the younger, was withdrawn. Tom didn't think of himself as part of a family; rather, he was one of five people held together, he said, "only by what I considered to be some kind of law. . . .

"I knew there were nice families out there where people loved each other and did nice things together," he said. "My best friend was a girl named Nancy. I loved being with her and her family. Her mother was so kind. 'Hi, kids, how would you like a cookie? Why don't you go in and listen to some music?' It was wonderful. I wanted to have that kind of family."

February 5, 1983

Someone I have loved dearly is dying of a disease that has descended on the gay community in this and other large coastal cities. It is predominantly, not totally, a gay problem, and I am writing a series of articles for the California *Voice* to try and sort out the facts and the myths about the disease. I hope the articles will quell some of the hysteria.

My friend, Clay Martin, is a wonderful human being. We've known each other for about seven or eight years. He owned a pet store across from my medical office on Collingwood in the Castro. I saw him every day and we delighted in each other's company.

We would have become lovers had we not both been involved in relationships at the time, me with Lee and he with Rich.

Clay and Rich moved to Key West a few years ago, and our contact was rare although we continued to love each other. Now he has AIDS, as does Rich, and Clay and I must not be intimate in any way for fear of contagion. I will do my best to let him know I am here for him, but how my heart aches to hold him and protect him.

Tom grew up in fear both of the Catholic Church, which he embraced, and of the Nazis, who haunted his early years and made him ashamed of his German ancestry. "I grew up guilty," he said, "a result of the Church influence and the Germanic. I believed in heaven and in hell, and everything pleasurable was evil or wrong. We were dirty, horrible creatures who constantly needed to guard against doing anything that would offend God."

Such lessons were drummed home at St. Michael's School in Paterson by a nun who inspired in Tom physical and emotional terror. She was a sadist, Tom said, who loved to punish errant boys, and to her all boys were errant. She once disciplined Tom by squeezing a door shut against his head. She would also rap her students' knuckles with a ruler.

During World War II, Tom and his classmates filled small Red Cross boxes with toothbrushes and toothpaste and soap and washcloths and Mercurochrome to send to poor and suffering children overseas.

Toward the end of the war, Tom saw a photograph in the New York *Daily News* of starving and bloated Japanese children strapped to their mothers' backs, scarred survivors of Hiroshima and Nagasaki, and he wondered what those children would do with toothbrushes and washcloths. "They don't have any teeth to brush," Tom told his teacher, "and there's no water to wash their faces."

"Who?" the nun asked.

"All those children," Tom said, "the ones who were hit with the atomic bomb."

"These boxes are not for the Japs!" the nun snapped. "They're for the poor children in Europe."

Japs. Krauts. Kikes. Niggers. The harsh names of his childhood assaulted Tom Flubacher, along with cruel plays upon his own name: Flumdunker. Flypaper. Flooziewatcher. The taunts stuck with him. So did images of blackouts and food rationing and atomic bombs raining down on Japan.

As the war ended, and both the threat of the Nazis and the influence of the Catholic Church diminished, Tom's fears faded and his life brightened. His parents had saved enough money to buy a store in Haledon from Tom's great-aunt, Emily Boeglin, or "Ma" Boeglin, as she was called by the youngsters who made her candy shop their hangout.

Ma Boeglin was in her eighties when she sold the store to the Flubachers, who converted it into a delicatessen and worked long hours. Marion Flubacher's salads were delicious, and the deli flourished. The Flubachers bought a Plymouth station wagon and a house in Wyckoff, a comfortable suburban village.

Tom's mother ran the deli, and his father, in addition to helping out there, drove a bus. Tom sought to turn them into a family. He liked to bring lunch to his dad and ride with him to the end of the line and back. Tom studied the faces of the people who rode the bus. Once he saw an old woman who looked so sad that Tom began to cry. He offered the woman a piece of fruit. "I wanted to make her smile," he said. "I liked that about me."

Years later, in one of the autobiographical short stories that he often started and sometimes finished, Tom called his central character "David Pippinger," and wrote of David's thirteenth birthday:

It was a season of muddy shoes and pollywogs.

David Pippinger was making his way along the railroad tracks, taking three or four ties at a time and occasionally walking on one of the tracks, counting the number of steps before he lost his balance, or measuring how far he could go without stepping off. It was one of the many little competitions he enjoyed with himself.

He was hungry and aware of the emptiness of his belly, but food was never so important to him that he would interrupt his fun to satisfy his hunger. But if he came across any wild fruit or berries, it mattered little if his stomach was full. He loved to eat wild things and he preferred their crisp tartness to the dull, soft sweetness of the cultivated fruit in the stores.

This was a special day for him. It was his thirteenth birthday. What was special was not that it was his birthday, but the number thirteen. This was to be a big step up for him, from childhood to something more important. He couldn't quite imagine if the world would change or he would change, but in any case there would be a difference and he welcomed it. He knew there would be some small celebration of the event when he got home, but he was in no hurry to get there.

His twelfth birthday was a vague memory. The only impression he had of it was the perfunctory performances of his parents. His brothers seemed not to acknowledge it as an event at all. He couldn't understand why it was so important to commemorate birthdays when it seemed that no one really cared about anyone's birthday but his own.

He remembered how hurt his mother felt when his older brother Jack forgot her birthday one year, and yet she ignored Jack's pain when one year she couldn't find the time to bake a cake for him.

David tightroped the rail across thirty-seven ties, his hands tucked into the pockets of his mackinaw. It made him feel like a hero. He imagined a small crowd of people applauding him as he stepped off the rail, a new world record added to his name.

He had a rather strong desire to be loved and admired.

The need to compete with himself, the desire to be loved and admired, all remained as strong in Tom as his taste for tart fruit.

February 6, 1983

Your mom invited Eric and Roger [Eric Wilkinson and Roger Tubb, two Englishmen who share an apartment they rent in Tom's house on Albion Street] and me to lunch at Artemis today. We discussed you, of course, and I put my hand on Mom's belly. I love doing that.

Later I went to see my friend Clay, and we talked about his approach to a disease that could be fatal to him at any moment. We also talked about you, and he shares with me the wonder of it all.

You may be a famous baby. Mom and I are trying to keep it quiet, but a child being born to Mom and me seems to be great news and generates a lot of speculation—and anxiety. There are those in the community who pretend to be horrified, but I think they secretly are glad. You will be watched, my child.

I hope Mom and I prepare you for the attitudes you may encounter. Perhaps all will be changed when you are old enough to know what an unusual situation we have placed you in. I have the feeling that you will handle it just fine. I love you.

Tonight the community celebrated itself at the annual Cable Car Awards. Chris is on the board and looked wonderful in her tuxedo—though her shoes were killing her.

There was a video of the Gay Games, and a rousing welcome to the athletes. The film showed Zohn presenting me with a medal for the javelin throw, and then we kissed. He was quite pleased and happy although we have been having problems in our relationship. But the love is there and I suspect it will conquer all.

I went on stage with Mom and the other athletes. People began shouting "Tom," and asking me to speak. I wasn't prepared, but managed a few words. (Eric tells me I never look anything but relaxed; I am, however, always very nervous about speaking.) In any case, it was exciting to feel the genuine good spirit that the Games have generated. The audience was in tears after the video.

Your Mom didn't receive the recognition she deserves. I will see to that in the future. She works so hard and contributes so much, she should be acknowledged and thanked appropriately by all the beneficiaries.

You are going into your third month. In about seven more, we meet face to face—oh happy day!

Tom Waddell's earliest glimpses of sex were harsh ones. Even before he entered his teens, his older brother, Arthur, introduced him to a secret club whose members practiced rather kinky rituals. One member had sex with his dog in front of the others. Tom was neither aroused nor amused.

Nor did he savor the impressions he gathered from an early-morning newspaper route that occasionally offered him the sights and sounds of crude and loveless sex. He saw men sodomize their wives, saw them strip off sagging condoms, saw wives recoil from the selfish demands of their husbands.

In his early teens, as one of a group of boys who called themselves the Main Street Gang, Tom had what he remembered as his first homosexual experience. One day several members of the gang rode their bikes to the nearby town of Wortendyke. They pedaled to the end of a dirt road, to a small house at the edge of the woods, and parked their bikes. Then, one at a time, the boys sneaked onto the porch at the side of the house.

"What's going on?" Tom asked.

"We're getting blow jobs," he was told by someone who had visited the house before.

Tom was the last to approach the man the boys called Wortendyke Willie, who lived with his mother and bestowed blow jobs on anyone who came to him. His face was always shrouded in darkness. None of the boys knew clearly what he looked like.

Sometimes, after the first experience, Tom returned alone to Wortendyke Willie's house. "It was exciting," he said, "and puzzling." Once, as he approached the house, bright lights suddenly flashed on, and a small band of policemen charged the porch as if they were storming an opium den. Tom dived to the ground, abandoned his bike, crept away and ran from the neighborhood, terrified of being caught and identified.

Later he went to the police station and reported that his bike had been stolen. He did not want the cops, or anyone else, to suspect he had been anywhere near the house in Wortendyke. "This is an illness," he told himself. "This isn't what I want to be. I'll outgrow it. Maybe." He fought against feelings of self-hatred.

One night when Tom was thirteen a schoolmate stayed at his house and suggested, "Let's play with each other."

It didn't sound like a bad idea to Tom. "Pretty soon," he remembered, "he was going down on me, and then he said, 'Do it to me, too.'"

Tom did. "I thought, *Am I going to die afterward?* Eventually we sixty-nined each other, but we never came in each other's mouth because somehow, in our weird way of reasoning, that would make us queers. One night he said, 'Why don't you make me come? Don't worry, I won't come in your mouth. I promise.'

"Strangely enough, he didn't. As he got close, he tapped me on the shoulder, withdrew, and spurted all over the place."

Tom did not see the other boy for a while. Then one day someone walked up to him at school and said, "I heard you gave ——— a blow job."

"I almost died," Tom said. "I thought I was going to die. I was so ashamed, and so hurt. I felt like I'd been betrayed."

Tom reacted quickly, and retaliated. "No," he said. "You've got it backwards. ——— gave *me* a blow job."

"All I could think was *Jesus, I'm going to be labeled a queer. My life is never going to be the same.* And then I thought, *I'm never going to do anything like that again. People can't be trusted.*"

Tom became increasingly aware of his sexual identity, his sexual preference. "I wasn't ready to admit it, not even to myself, but I knew I was a homosexual. It wasn't a label. It was a feeling. The things that hit me in the groin always seemed so different from the things that hit everyone else.

"But who could I talk to?

"Not to my priest. He would've condemned me.

"Not to my older brother. He would've killed me.

"Not to my parents. We didn't communicate or share feelings. I couldn't go to them and say, 'Gee, I'm having these really strange feelings.' They might've sent me to a psychiatrist, maybe, but that wasn't what I needed. What I needed was someone to say to me, 'You're OK.' "

Tom used to watch television at a friend's home. He remembered seeing Hopalong Cassidy on an old Admiral console. He also recalled seeing his friend's father walk into the room nude. "My eyes practically jumped out of my head. I kept stealing glances. It did strange things to me. I thought, *I'm really bizarre.*"

Tom's own father was not so accommodating. Once when the Flubachers took a rare family trip, to New England, they all stayed in a single hotel room. When they changed into their swimsuits, Elmer did so behind a chair, and Tom wondered why. "Once my father caught me looking at him undressing, and he got very angry. I thought nudity really was a very bad thing. I thought I was the only person in the world who felt the way I felt."

Inevitably, Tom drifted away from his parents and his brothers, envying his friends for their homes. "I desperately wanted the feeling of having a family. Like Roger Durant's family, so loving, so warm, always laughing and kidding. Roger used to wrestle with his dad. I wish I could have wrestled with mine. I *knew* that someday I would have a family and I would have children and they would feel loved."

February 8, 1983

I am very depressed these days, trying to put Gay Games II into focus and determine my role in them. The house is chaotic, and my books and papers are scattered all over the place. Zohn is in pain over our relationship, and I find myself creeping up to my room (which will one day be yours) for solace and solitude.

I always view depression as a natural thing. It is a falling back, a gathering time, a time to reflect and plan and examine. I will remain like this, as is my pattern, silent and uncomplaining, until some revelation or inspiration strikes me.

Eric and Roger are very understanding and, as always, concerned. They are wonderful, and I'm glad they will be in your life.

Tomorrow Mom and I play racquetball. I haven't done any exercise for weeks, and I've been smoking cigarettes—not a good combination for me. Exercise has always been my form of meditation. I draw great strength from it, physically as well as emotionally and intellectually. I will get back—and perhaps tomorrow will be the start.

The Flubacher family fell apart. Arthur stole cars, drank heavily, became addicted to amphetamines, pep pills. "He was a terrible person," Tom said. "When he died of a heart attack, I didn't go to his funeral." Tom felt no closer to Richard. "He grew more and more quiet," Tom said. His mother spent time in a sanatorium, struggling with tuberculosis.

Tom sensed that his mother wanted more out of life, more than she had known in her marriage to Elmer Flubacher. She wanted excitement and variety. "What she was saying," Tom said, "although not out loud, was, *God, there's got to be more than this. I'm not going to live this way.* Dad was perfectly happy just having a house, a bed, a wife, a meal. Mom was more of an adventurer."

The marriage—without passion, never more than a union of convenience—collapsed. Strangely, Tom was devastated. "It can't happen," he told himself. "My parents can't divorce." He decided he wouldn't allow them to, and persuaded a priest to talk to Elmer and Marion. Waiting outside, he overheard the priest scolding his mother, angrily calling her a whore.

Tom fled, crying, his faith in the Church, already frayed, now shattered. Elmer Flubacher said he would move away. "You'll be with your mom and your brothers," he told Tom.

"Dad, please don't go," Tom begged. "Stay here. I'll live with you."

For a while, they shared an apartment, and Tom was happy. Often he and his father ate out together. Tom loved to order salads that reminded him of the ones his mother made. But they were never quite as good.

Marion Flubacher eventually remarried twice and settled in Florida. Tom and his father moved in again with Tom's grandparents, and when Elmer Flubacher began dating his ex-wife's best friend and, in time, married her, Tom once again felt unloved, unneeded, unwanted. He reached out for new friends, people with whom he could be comfortable, and he found them in Hazel and Gene Waddell.

Tom met the Waddells during his early teens and was immediately attracted to them. They had no children of their own. They were former vaudevillians, Gene an acrobat and Hazel a dancer; they had even played the Palace, not as headliners but as a supporting act, comedy tumblers. Even earlier, Gene had belonged to a troupe called The Three Jacksons, who performed daredevil acrobatic feats. Once they staged their act on the ledge of the balcony on the eighty-sixth floor of the Empire State Building, more than a thousand feet above Fifth Avenue. That was before Tom was born, but he loved to watch the newsreel coverage of the Jacksons' daring performance. The sight of Gene Waddell doing a high-risk handstand could make him laugh even in the last weeks before his death.

February 12, 1983

Zohn has been very angry lately because he feels insecure and unloved. I don't think this is a result of his actually *being* unloved. This is a problem with a lot of people—who have not learned to love themselves first. When you love yourself, then your security lies within and makes it easier to love others.

Hazel and Gene Waddell lived perhaps half a mile from Tom's home in Wyckoff, and Tom used to run from his house to theirs. He loved to run everywhere.

He mowed the lawn for the Waddells and helped Gene work on the Red Barn studio that he was constructing for Hazel's dance classes. In return Gene taught Tom tumbling, and Hazel taught him ballet.

"I liked dancing," Tom said. "I liked motion. I liked the finiteness of the movements in ballet, the fact that there was historical significance to each move, the fact that each move had its own name. I loved the grace and the beauty and the discipline. I loved to choreograph dances for myself so that I could run and jump and spin."

For Tom, dancing was an adventure, and an escape—sometimes.

He and his older brother shared a newspaper-delivery route, and Arthur, who drove the truck, did not think much of Tom's ballet lessons.

"You faggot," Arthur called his brother one day.

"Step out of the truck," Tom said.

Arthur got out, but before he could attack, Tom punched him in the face. "I think I broke his nose. And then I ran. I was faster than him. I had no more problems with him, but we were never friends. Funny. Years later, when I told him I was gay, he just shrugged. He didn't care one way or the other."

Tom was beginning to feel comfortable with his emerging feelings. "I liked myself," he said. "I really did like myself. I liked who I was. I liked what I felt. I didn't want to change any of that.

"But I didn't want to be this physical, social, bizarre outcast. I wanted to be liked. I wanted to have lots of friends, and

I realized the way I was going to do that was not through my intellectual capacities, because I didn't feel I had any at the time, but through my athletic abilities, and that came very easily to me.

"I threw myself into sports to compensate for my feelings."

February 18, 1983

Zohn is going away for several months—with his friend Jim Hormel. They are going to Paris, Venice, then the Greek islands. Zohn is quite unhappy with his life, and it is our relationship that is forcing him to think of changes. He lives in the fast lane with great bursts of activity and lots of drugs, but he is a remarkable man with great integrity and love and I am certain that he will return with safe and sane alternatives in his life. I certainly want him to be part of mine—and ours.

Tom dedicated himself to sports for a variety of reasons. In the first place, he loved the sheer physicality, the effort, the sweat, the feeling of accomplishment. He joined the track team at Ramsey High School, and he sensed a kinship between the sport and ballet. "Track and field has that same kind of beauty," he said. "Whether it's a jeté or a world record in the high jump doesn't make any difference. Here's someone propelling his body through the air to achieve a particular effect."

He also knew that his participation in sports was a credential—and, he readily admitted, "I always collected credentials." In football, for instance, he found that if he knocked down a few people, he acquired a certain prestige and acceptance.

Perhaps most important, sports were his cover, his shield.

On the field he was one of the guys, one of the jocks, and was automatically considered macho—ironic considering how many athletes, Tom eventually discovered, were also gay.

"I really wanted to be a dancer," Tom said, "but who were the dancers in the fifties? They were 'faggots.' It was not something I wanted to be identified with at the time. It was too threatening, too frightening. There was a stigma. I didn't want to be 'a homosexual.' I wanted to be a person.

"I'm a little ashamed now that I didn't pursue dancing more vigorously, that I didn't commit myself to it. But I didn't have enough courage then, enough confidence." Edward Villella and Jacques D'Amboise, both brilliant ballet dancers and both straight, were not prominent enough to soften the stigma that afflicted their art.

Tom moved in with the Waddells in his mid-teens, loved them, and lived his life with them. Hazel scolded him, prodded him, taught him French, forced him to study, introduced him to artichokes and to affection. *God, they care,* Tom thought with some amazement. *They really care about me.*

For the first time in his life he felt like part of a family. There was nothing he enjoyed more than sitting on their front porch with Gene and Hazel, listening to their stories, sharing their memories. "It was an oasis. Here were two people who had traveled all over the world, who had stories to tell. I would sit and listen to them for hours, fascinated."

He joined in shows with the Waddells, polishing his own acrobatic act in the process. "I liked what it was doing for my coordination, my legs, my strength. I felt springier, more powerful. I got other football players involved, which was fine, until I tried to get them interested in ballet, too. That was too much. I had gone too far. Their parents didn't like that. They were macho assholes."

Still, Tom worked on his own balletic skills, and progressed to the point where Hazel told him, "I can't teach you any more. I've taught you all I know. If you want to learn more, you've got to go to New York to study." So twice a week he traveled to Manhattan for ballet classes.

"Then one day," he said, "as I was getting undressed, another male dancer, who was very effeminate, came over to me and grabbed my cock and said, 'Hey, anytime you want that played with, just let me know.' I was in shock. I got dressed, went home, and never went back.

"I didn't want to be like that. I didn't want to be effeminate. At that time homosexuals were generally thought of as men who wanted to be women. But I didn't want to be a woman. I liked being male. I liked feeling male. I liked having hair on my chest and hair on my chin. I liked having muscles and strength. I was bothered by the idea that gayness meant femininity. I was confused by it, too."

February 25, 1983

I put my hand on Mom's bare belly today. We had lunch together at Artemis. I hadn't seen Mom for about a week. She had been to Lake Tahoe for a vacation. She stayed up late, glued to the gambling tables. She goes at gambling like she does everything else—all the way. I hope you experienced it with Mom. There's a lot of energy and excitement involved in gambling.

Mom is still projecting some hostility my way. It's not me she is angry with, it's my being a male. It's very understandable—her sense of oppression by the male—but I need to remind her that I'm as much a feminist as she is and convince her that the best way to handle this anger is to channel it into educating men. The best way to educate anyone is to do it lovingly, reasonably and, if you really mean business, with a sense of humor.

And men need to be educated. They need to de-condition themselves from what they've been taught to be and think.

This will happen through education via the process of discovery. Put out an invitation for friendship and warmth and try somehow to touch the other person (in as many ways as you can "touch" someone). Not all will respond because many have fears about intimacy, but some will respond and will let you in and will learn from you. Invariably, they will have something to teach you as well, even if it's only a new way to teach. We learn by teaching.

My child, whatever is happening to you now, I press my feelings your way in the hope that there may be a part of you that is receptive to them. Surely you must feel your mother's power and love (I call this "soul"), and I hope mine can join hers to make you feel like the miracle you are.

Mom is going into the fourth month with you. I look at her and I want to burst with happiness—while at the same moment I feel inhibited and a bit fearful that we will not be as synergistic toward you as I would wish. I want to be much closer to Mom, but it may take a long time.

I contemplate and rejoice in your arrival. Mom asked me to come over on Sunday to go over your room. She has a list of things to do and to get for you. How I love it when she asks me to do these things.

I may paint your room.

Clearly, Tom was a boy's boy, a man's man—curious phrases, capable of being read several ways—daring, competitive, powerful. In the summers he would race to the highest diving board and perform the most demanding dives, from flips to backward somersaults. "I was always attracted to things that scared me," Tom said. "I was always attracted to danger. And it wasn't that I *wanted* to do those dives. I *had to*. I felt I had no choice."

He was one of the best athletes in his school, but he was never *the* best, never the big star, never so outstanding he would be spoiled by adulation, never so spectacular that anyone dreamed he would someday represent the United States in the Olympic Games. Tom wasn't even the best end on the Ramsey High football team. His friend Roger Durant was better, honorable mention on the All-County team.

As much as Tom liked competing, liked playing, he disliked the sports *system* in high school, the emphasis on winning, on winners. He seethed when coaches berated mediocre athletes, cringed when anyone's efforts were demeaned. At times he thought about punching the offending coaches— violent retribution, an echo of his upbringing in the Church.

Once he became an athlete, the subject of homosexuality almost never came up—when someone did remark to him, years after the incident, "I heard you once gave ——— a blow job," Tom responded, in eloquent jockspeak, "Bullshit!"—yet even though he was never again confronted, he always feared that people knew, or at least suspected, that his sexual preference wasn't conventional. He kept his feelings, and his fears, to himself. It was his secret. After his first experience, that numbing betrayal, he confided in no one.

He was a well-mannered young man, polite, pleasant, likable. "People liked me, I thought, mostly because of athletics," Tom said. "Nobody ever said I was really bright or really funny. They just said I was really nice."

He dated some of the more attractive girls in his high school, but he didn't play the sexual mind-and-body games his contemporaries enjoyed. "The object, I think, was to get the girls to some fever pitch, to some point of no return. The theory was that unless you got them to that point, they weren't going to be interested in sex, they weren't going to acquiesce. The whole idea was to win, to conquer. I never understood why people couldn't touch each other just because they liked each other and liked to touch each other.

"Necking was so tedious, so uninteresting. *To me.* What I

really wanted was a wholesome relationship—with another man. Of course I had been told that there was no such thing as 'a wholesome relationship' with a member of the same sex."

March 3, 1983

Your mother and I had dinner out last night after seeing "Victor, Victoria." We ate at the Cliff House during a storm.

We played racquetball today—Mom and I and you. Mom won two out of three from me, but I'm catching up to her. We both play hard—and to win. She has slowed up carrying you, which is a little unfair, but we're both competitors. You will realize that as you get to know us.

In his high school yearbook, next to the name of Tom Flubacher, there is a picture of a young man with a pompadour, a bold bow tie, a vest that aspired to match the bow tie, and an open grin. His teenage biography reads like that of an all-American boy, up to a point: "Tom . . . tall . . . strawberry blond and friendly . . . likes hamburgers smothered in onions and all sports . . . dislikes homework, loud cars, losing games . . . enjoys eating chow mein and playing football . . . plans to be a commercial dancer."

Tom was bold enough to confess his desire to be a dancer, but he was not bold enough to follow through. He wanted to go to college, but his grades—mostly C's and D's—barely qualified him. He had, however, set a Ramsey High School record by high-jumping five feet ten inches, and the track coach, Gordon Bedford, was a Springfield (Mass.) College graduate. Bedford recommended Tom to the Springfield track coach, Vern Cox, and Cox offered Tom a scholarship.

Tom did not apply to any other college. He decided he would go to Springfield, which was known for its physical-education curriculum, and major in phys ed and become a coach. But he would not be like most coaches. He would be sensitive, tolerant of an athlete's limitations. He would not stress winning above all else.

March 20, 1983

I have been traveling, speaking about the Gay Games. I spoke to the Western Conference of Gay Students at Sacramento State University and to the Dorian Group in Seattle.

The Games are not just about athletics. They are about bringing people together in a spirit of love and friendship and cooperation. When we participate together, we discover each other and that leads to greater understanding and tolerance.

This is the period of the AIDS crisis, which is a deadly disease syndrome that is affecting gay men predominantly. I write articles on the subject for the California *Voice* and I am trying to bring some common sense to the crisis and offer people ways to begin to alter their behavior in the least traumatic way.

We are proud at Springfield College to have wedded this Greek ideal of physical and mental fitness to the Biblical ideal of moral and spiritual fitness.
—Dr. Glenn A. Olds
President, Springfield College

Tom Waddell fell in love in college. He fell in love *with* college. "Springfield became my new family," he said. "I loved the people there. I loved everything that was going on."

Like many young men, Tom found himself in college. He discovered exactly who he was: "I was a jock. That was my identity, and I was comfortable with it."

Tom was a jock in a jock school.

In 1891 a young Springfield College faculty member named James Naismith tacked up a peach basket, handed his students a large round ball, and invented a game he called basketball.

Four years later one of Naismith's former Springfield students, William Morgan, put up a net, handed *his* students a large round ball, and invented a game he called volleyball.

A century later, volleyball and basketball were two of the most popular sports in the world. Not bad for a small school in western Massachusetts.

By the late 1950s Tom was one of close to 1,200 undergraduate and graduate students at Springfield, roughly a fourth of them women. More than half of the students were enrolled in the School of Physical Education.

The Springfield soccer team was the national collegiate cochampion in 1957. Springfield's Bill Yorzyck was the only American man to earn a gold medal in swimming in the 1956 Olympic Games in Melbourne, Australia; Yorzyck won the 100-meter butterfly. One of Tom's teammates on the Springfield football team, Dick MacPherson, went on to coach Syracuse University and then the New England Patriots.

Today Springfield accommodates more than 2,000 students, and the Basketball Hall of Fame is situated on the edge of the campus, with the Volleyball Hall of Fame not far away. Springfield College also has its own athletic Hall of Fame, which honors, among others, James Naismith, William Morgan, and, after considerable controversy, Tom Waddell.

Sports at Springfield offered Tom protection, a sense of security. "I think a lot of men go into athletics for the same reason I did—a need to prove their maleness. They're fighting what they perceive to be feminine qualities—sensitivity, perhaps, or a desire to paint or play the piano—so they have to establish a sense of masculinity."

He was not suggesting that all athletes are gay. "I never encountered one person at Springfield College whom I even suspected of being a homosexual.

"Of course, I don't think anyone suspected me of being a homosexual, either. I certainly never told anyone."

May 20, 1983

Mom and I went away the past two days. We drove to Lake Tahoe—just to be together and to have some fun at the casinos. Mom is quite big now.

The first sport in which Tom excelled at Springfield was gymnastics. Thanks to the lessons from Gene Waddell, he had a head start. He was both a competitor and a performer, engaging in dual meets against such schools as Penn State and Temple and West Point, and traveling with an exhibition squad that blended gymnastics and entertainment.

"Tom was the star of those shows," said Frank Wolcott, the Springfield gymnastics coach who codirected the exhibition team. "He could dance, and he was very athletic. And, of course, he loved to be in front of an audience."

A typical exhibition program included, besides performances on the parallel bars and the flying rings and the side horse, displays of rope climbing and Indian club swinging and pyramid building, juxtaposed with such vaudevillian routines as the Charleston, in straw hats and striped blazers, and the Old Soft Shoe, in derbies and bow ties. Tom starred in both numbers.

He performed spectacularly in competition, too. "Gymnastics is both physical exercise and artistic performance," suggested Ellis H. Champlin, the director of the School of

Physical Education, and Tom embraced both disciplines and thrived on them. He was New England champion on the flying rings.

By his sophomore year Tom and his closest friend at the time, his roommate Don Marshman, were costars of the gymnastics team. They were known on campus as "The Gold Dust Twins." Marshman, a premed student, was New England champion on the trampoline.

Marshman's family lived on an apple farm not far from Springfield, and Tom enjoyed their hospitality and warmth. "I loved Don," Tom said. "I loved him to death. He was a beautiful person, and he was smart—and *he* liked me. That was neat, that someone special like Don could like me. He had a wonderful girlfriend named Jeannie, and the three of us were inseparable. We went skiing and camping together.

"I had no physical feelings for Don. I loved him as a person. I loved his dedication to medicine, his desire to become a doctor and to heal people and help them."

One day Tom and Don were working out together in the gym. Don was recovering from the flu, trying to get his muscles and reflexes back in shape. He was on the flying rings, preparing to dismount at the end of a giant swing, when, weakened by his illness, he lost his grip, sailed beyond the cushioning mats and crashed to the floor headfirst.

"He looked at me," Tom said, "and he had a look of terror on his face, and then he went blank."

Tom rushed to Don's side and cradled him in his arms. He saw blood trickling from Don's ear. His neck was cracked. He was rushed to the hospital, where doctors operated on him that night. But the next morning Don Marshman died.

Tom went back to the apartment he and Don had shared, and for a few days he refused to come out. "Our landlady, a kind woman, brought me food," Tom said. Then a friend persuaded him to step out, to come to his apartment and sit in a large bathtub and try to relax, to unwind. "Just soak," the friend said, and Tom did.

Tom was one of the pallbearers at Don's funeral.

Don was nineteen. It was Tom's first close encounter with death.

.

Years later when Bill Toomey, Tom's Olympic teammate and friend and rival, found himself incapable of accepting Tom's homosexuality, unable to grasp its reality, he tried to explain it away by saying, "Tom's not a homosexual, he's just very sensitive. He had a close friend who died when they were in college, and I think the friend's death had a great impact on Tom."

Tom knew that Bill was simply trying to place his sexual orientation in a context he could fathom. Yes, Don's death did have a great impact on Tom, but not in the way Toomey imagined.

"From then on," Tom said, "I began thinking seriously about becoming a doctor. I switched from physical education to a premed course."

July 31, 1983

Long time since writing. It's been a strange time in my life and the anticipation of your arrival has had a great deal to do with it. It's interesting how my thoughts have altered over the past few months: from romantic fantasies about our new family to serious concerns about our welfare.

The changes have not been unpleasant, but they are certainly sobering. Serious business this is, starting a family—plus the added elements of who and what we are.

Your arrival was celebrated yesterday in a unique ceremony held at Jim Hormel's and Larry Dean Soule's home. They, and Chris and Zohn, had a baby shower in your honor and invited my friends as well as Mom's. It was a celebration that will be remembered for a long time; in fact, there was a video made of the gift opening. I have a feeling you'll enjoy seeing it some day.

One thing is certain: You will have many friends as you grow up. Having you in our lives is a great departure for our circle of people. Most of us have formed extended families because so many of us have been rejected by our primary relatives. And now your Mom and I have introduced an entirely new element into our collective lifestyles. While your anticipated arrival has been met with great joy and happiness and support from all our friends, it has also been met with mixed feelings of confusion and anxiety.

Being openly gay at this particular time in history is very exciting, but it also means there are many doors to open and new paths to follow. We are all struggling to be understood by the dominant society.

I am on a plane going to Vancouver, Canada. I am to speak at the closing ceremonies of the first Vancouver Gay Summer Games. There is a great movement afoot in the form of organized gay athletic events. This is a positive statement of the quality of our lives, and the events bring great visibility and identity. We are on a threshold and we are moving cautiously in this new arena. Our politics and our highly-publicized lifestyles (and our diseases) have propelled us into the public eye as never before, and we are fighting against popular, but negative, stereotypes. These various competitions provide an alternative view of what we are all about.

I will tell you unabashedly that the first Games were my idea—a very idealistic notion that had been growing in my head for many years. I simply had to wait for the proper time and inspiration for it to happen.

Your Mom, Uncles Zohn and Eric, Aunt Chris and others I will tell you about all had their hands in the success of these first Games. We have become a formidable team, and we have much work to do in the future.

Tom always preferred the sports that emphasized finesse, grace, and technique, like gymnastics and track and field. But, he admitted, "There's part of me that's real animal. When I play basketball, I like a rough body-contact game. I don't want to play a 'faggot' game."

During his junior year in college Tom turned his toughness once again to football. "I was just as aggressive and hostile as anybody else," he said. "I loved knocking people down. I liked running over people. The whole thing was fun."

Almost the whole thing. "I hated *getting* hit," Tom confessed, a distaste he shared with even all-pro football players. "But I loved the camaraderie of football, and I loved catching the ball."

Tom was a wide receiver, a pass-catching end, and the highlight of his football career came during a home game against the University of Connecticut, which had just announced that it would no longer play Springfield, that it was upgrading its schedule to compete against bigger schools with more talented teams.

Spurred by the insult, Springfield stunned Connecticut's Huskies, 19–14, and Tom scored the decisive touchdown, the target of a fifty-yard pass thrown by Les "Porky" Plumb, who earned honorable mention as a quarterback on the small-college Little All-American team. Plumb called the play and sent Tom sprinting straight downfield.

"He let it fly," Tom said, "and I was running with my arms stretched out in front of me, and as I approached the goal line, I was on the verge of collapsing."

Then Tom made a spectacular move. "I didn't exactly

dive," he said. "I sort of fell. As I reached the goal line, I fell and I looked up and the ball landed in my hands. I was stretched across the goal line, and I held on to the ball."

"It was one of the most unusual catches I ever saw," said Ted Dunn, an assistant who became the head coach at Springfield the following year.

It was the last time Springfield beat Connecticut. Tom received honorable mention on the All-East team that week. "It made me a football hero," he said, "which was something I never expected."

The following week, as a reward for his heroics, Tom was moved into the starting lineup, against Amherst, a formidable opponent. "When I heard I was starting, I said, 'Oh, no.' I got hurt the first play of the game."

Tom did not try out for the team as a senior. He rested on his laurel.

August 2, 1983

The trip to Vancouver was an astounding success. The airfare was paid by the Vancouver Gay Summer Games Committee. I spoke at their awards banquet and had many conversations with the committee members. It's a beautiful and friendly city and would be an ideal site for Gay Games III in 1990. I tried to encourage them to make a bid.

The following day, I rode in an open car which had my name and "title" on its side. It was Vancouver's annual Gay Pride parade. We ended up at a park where I spoke along with a number of political leaders, including a member of the Canadian Parliament.

Later, at a picnic for all the participants, I was interviewed on TV and pushed my philosophy of using athletics as the supreme tool to get people together for a positive purpose, to include *all* people regardless of their race, gender, sexual preference and, of course, regardless of their nationality. The Games' purpose is to minimize those aspects of our lives and get people to cooperate and have fun together. All in all, it was a fine weekend and profitable in terms of gaining adherents to the notion of what the Games are all about.

I got no sleep that night, but made my way back to my host's home, woke him up and went straight to the airport and on to New York, where I was met by Stanley Perlo. We went to his parents' home in Croton-on-Hudson, old friends and fine people. Stanley's father, Victor, is a well-known member of the American Communist Party. He and his wife Ellen are active contributors to the *Daily World*, which is the official CP newspaper.

Now I am at The Farm in Great Barrington, Massachusetts, with Enge, seeing my friends of many years, friends who have really become my family. They all know I am gay and they know that I have a special attachment to Enge. It doesn't seem to matter how frequently or infrequently I come to The Farm, we all love each other and we are all loyal.

Enge is nearing the end of his life. He has been the center of all our lives for about as long as anyone can remember. Now he is very old (88), difficult and crotchety.

I am here instead of with Mom because I fear Enge will die soon. He has been my family for many years and I am grateful to him for influencing my life in so many wonderful ways. Though he has changed, I love him and will always cherish him and his memory.

This farmhouse is an important part of my life, as is Enge. I first came here in 1959 to apply for a summer job as a counselor. The boys' camp was owned by Pete and Sarah Menaker. I took the job and had one of the most enjoyable summers I can remember.

Camp To-Ho-Ne is for middle-class intellectual Jewish kids—and I learned more from them than they learned from me. I did, however, bring sports into their lives in a way they had never experienced before.

Enge Menaker, Pete's younger brother, and Glen, Enge's friend and partner of many years, ran the guest camp, which was mostly for very progressive and leftist intellectuals. I not only got a supreme education on all topics, but I was accepted into their circle as a family member and that was one of the most secure situations I've ever felt.

I also fell in love with Enge, who for the rest of my life is the single most important person. No matter what happens to me from this day on, there is simply no way I can experience a more profound love than I had with Enge.

I've loved other people and have felt loved by others—and I imagine that you and I will have a remarkable and unique loving relationship—but it will be different!

Enge and I felt no age barrier and our love was as physical as it was emotional and intellectual. I'm sure I will tell you much about him as you grow up. How I wish he will live long enough to meet you. He is a great man.

He is very old now and seems unhappy with his life. His friend of many years, Glen, died of lung cancer in 1963 and it was very traumatic for Enge. I think in many ways a part of Enge died with him.

I have been visiting with all my special friends up here. They, of course, know that I am gay and that your Mom is, too, but they have no judgments about such things. I admire them and think they do me as well. You are often the topic of discussion. They want to know all about Mom and how we met, how we intend to raise you, what are our arrangements, etc. They are genuinely pleased for me and anxious to meet Mom and you. Perhaps we'll come this way next year when you are able to make the trip.

One thing is certain: You will have many friends to visit here on the East Coast—in New York, New Jersey, Florida and Massachusetts.

Football allowed Tom to explore his more aggressive athleticism, and offered him a small taste of fame. Gymnastics indulged the pure showman in him, and brought him his first brush with tragedy. But it was track and field that rewarded the pure athlete in Tom, and lifted him to his greatest triumph. Vernon Cox, who spent more than forty years at Springfield as coach and athletic director, called Tom "the best all-around track person I ever coached."

Tom started as a specialist, a high jumper, attracted to that event by its grace as well as its physical demands. He used the Western roll, curling his body over the bar, first one leg, then the other. This was the standard technique for high jumpers until, during the 1960s, an American named Dick Fosbury slid headfirst, backward, over the bar and so introduced the Fosbury Flop. "The Western roll was such a beautiful jump," Tom, the purist, maintained. "It was poetic. There was nothing very attractive about the Fosbury Flop."

As a college junior, Tom set a high-jump record for the Eastern Intercollegiate Conference, leaping six feet five and one-quarter inches. But by the time he was a senior, he was so versatile and skilled he was almost a one-man track team. Tom came within a point, in fact, of winning a dual meet all by himself. When Springfield beat Amherst—108½–26½—Tom alone collected twenty-six points. He finished first in the high jump, the long jump, the high hurdles and the javelin, and second in the shot put and the discus.

Dick Wotruba, a decathlete at Holy Cross College in nearby Worcester, Massachusetts, watched Tom compete and was impressed as much by his versatility as by his skill. "Look, you're already doing six or seven events," Wotruba said. "Why don't you just pick up a few more and we'll train together?"

So Tom added the 100-meter dash, the pole vault, the low hurdles, and the 1,500-meter run to his athletic repertoire and became a decathlete—one of a very special breed that dates back to 1912, when an American Sack and Fox Indian named

Jim Thorpe won the first Olympic decathlon and was told by his royal host, King Gustav V of Sweden, "Sir, you are the greatest athlete in the world." To which Thorpe, according to legend, responded, "Thanks, King."

Ever since, the Olympic decathlon champion has been called, with some though certainly not total justification, the world's greatest athlete.

Tom Waddell was no Thorpe, neither on the football field nor on the track—Thorpe was an all-American in football, and outdid Tom's performance against Amherst by once winning six events and outscoring the entire Lafayette College team in a dual meet—but, then again, no one was.

Tom polished his varied skills by working out regularly with Wotruba. "When they trained," Vern Cox recalled, "it was like a two-man track meet."

Like many decathletes, even Olympic champions, Tom experienced his greatest difficulty in the pole vault; the proper technique always eluded him. "I used the 'steel' technique," Tom said, "even after I started using a fiberglass pole. It was hilarious to watch me vault." It was also painful. "It ruined my shoulders."

Still, by the summer of 1960, at the end of a postgraduate year at Springfield and in only his second year as a decathlete, Tom recorded the nineteenth-highest score in the world. He accumulated 6,945 points in the U.S. national championships, performing particularly well in the long jump (24 feet 5¾ inches), the javelin (220 feet 1½ inches), and the most torturous event, the 1,500-meter run (4:43.2). He finished eighth in one of the most dramatic decathlon competitions ever. His friend Wotruba came in twelfth. UCLA's Rafer Johnson was first, defeating his good friend and great rival, C. K. Yang, both men breaking the world record. A few months later, Johnson and Yang again finished 1–2, this time in the Olympic Games in Rome.

In 1960 Tom found himself for the first time in the company of elite world-class athletes. He met Al Oerter, the extraordinary discus thrower who would become the first man to win the same track-and-field event in four consecutive Olympic Games. "I felt like a little kid," Tom said. "I was in awe of Al Oerter. He remained a hero to me for a quarter of a century."

He couldn't have imagined then that he and Oerter would one day be Olympic teammates. He thought his own track-and-field career was, for all practical purposes, finished in 1960.

"Tom was a remarkable athlete," one of his track-and-field teammates at Springfield, Jack Savoia, once said. "He took such pleasure in practicing, in improving, in doing his best. He was an inspiration to me."

That remained one of Tom's greatest gifts—his ability to inspire others.

August 3, 1983

It's getting close to your arrival and I am anxious to get home to be near Mom. I carry a picture of her with me and I look at it often.

What will you look like? What will you be—boy or girl? I have no preference. I just want you to be healthy.

I had a long conversation with my old and dear friend Jackie Leonard. She and her husband Hank are like family to me. They helped me financially through medical school and we are very close. They have three children, who now also have children. Perhaps you will get to know Katy and Michael; they will be about your age.

Jackie is a psychologist and a very bright woman. I asked her what I should do to be a good father (I've been reading Piaget's theories, which she teaches), and she told me not to worry, I just need to let you know that I love you—and she felt certain that I would do that.

Your Mom is going to be such a good mother. I have visions of our family doing all sorts of wonderful things together as we watch you grow.

I sometimes worry that my age (I am now 45, but I feel like 20) will be a problem. I do want to play with you and be available to do vigorous things such as play sports and climb mountains. When you are 15, I will be 60—perhaps you will feel I am an old man. There is the possibility I will die before you are old enough to be on your own, but Mom is young and will see you well along. I just pray that we have the opportunity to get to know each other.

The world is changing rapidly. There are many things to fear and many things that need attention from responsible citizens. But there is also much beauty in the world and I hope there is time to give you the benefit of my experiences with beauty.

There is the world of music. Eric, Roger, Mom and Zohn are all aware of its magic and power. There is the world of art and theater, of sport and dance (the two are synonymous to me). So many things to appreciate and enjoy.

So many people become self-centered to the point of ignoring all the delights of this world. Many people you meet will be low on self-esteem and they will be trapped into seeking some kind of security. Others will be secure and they will go outside of themselves and realize that between the miracle of birth and the ultimate experience of death, there is a lifetime to be lived.

If ever you are despondent or feeling lonely, or not liking yourself, please read these words again and, for me and Mom, but mostly for yourself, go outside of yourself and allow all the beauty to come in.

You will, no doubt, have your heartaches and your own problems. I hope we prepare you to handle them in a satisfactory way. It is perfectly normal to feel sad, or hurt, but you must not let those feelings overwhelm you so that you cannot appreciate the wonder of the experience of living.

We have so much to talk about. I can hardly wait for you.

I do know that for the first three years Mom and I will be right by your side, feeding you, changing your diapers, drying your tears and sharing your laughter. You will be so vulnerable and we will be so omnipotent. As you grow older, you will begin to be your own complete person and you will become independent and responsible for yourself.

I hope this journal will be a comfort for you and give evidence to the fact that you were conceived out of love, that what we want from the event is to give you the tools and the opportunity to make your lifetime a wondrous experience.

I do have a selfish hope, and I will be careful not to express it to the point of discouraging it, but I would hope that you would view your life as an opportunity to also make the world a better place for future generations. There are many ways of doing that which are very satisfying and rewarding.

Tom Waddell entered Springfield College a virgin—with women—and graduated with his virtue intact. "I never had a sexual experience with anyone from the college, and I was there five years," he said. But he did make an effort.

Once he found himself in bed with a woman who told him she wanted very much to consummate their relationship. "I panicked," Tom recalled. "I said, 'We're not married, it wouldn't be right, let's wait, this is wrong, et cetera, et cetera.' Bullshit!

"I was telling her, 'No, we can't have sex, it's not right.' But sometimes, walking to my room at night, I'd get picked up by guys in their forties and fifties, married guys, *queers*, cruising, looking for somebody's cock to suck. I'd never reciprocate. That would make me what they were. But I'd let them give me a blow job."

Tom was still struggling with his instincts, still entertaining the thought that his preference might change. And he did, in fact, find a girl he wanted to have sex with, *dreamed* of having sex with. "We got really close," he said, "and she turned it off: 'Oh, God, no. I'm afraid of getting pregnant.'"

But even if she had said yes, it probably would not have changed Tom's life.

August 29, 1983

It is now 3:30 in the morning. My dear child, you are so much on my mind these days, and I am so worried.

Mom is due any day now, and she is being checked out at the hospital every day because there is some concern about toxemia. I don't think there is any *real* concern, but Mom is being cautious.

I've been in the hospital, too. Eight days ago, I began to have severe pains in my left side and groin. They were most excruciating and unremitting and I suspected I was passing a kidney stone. After a few minutes of anguish, I had Eric drive me to the emergency room at Kaiser where I was admitted. I didn't get out until yesterday, after seven days of nightmare pain, and, of course, I was horrified at the thought of being in the hospital delivering a renal stone just when your mother was delivering you.

I am feeling a terrible distance between your mother and me. It's as though she's thinking that I'm creating every kind of conceivable crisis to avoid your arrival. She has the tendency to think of me as she does "the guys," and I get lumped into that heap.

She and I agreed upon and co-signed an agreement about your childhood and our individual and collective responsibility.

Mom will have custody. Her great fear was somehow losing that. I suppose it's a real consideration, but I am disappointed that she ever imagined it would be a real possibility.

I have been paying half your Mom's rent and utilities for almost a year now and also give her extra money when I can (since I am not working for any remuneration for almost two years now). She said she lost some time working while she was carrying you and asked if I would help her make it up, so I gave her another $1,000 out of my savings. We also share other expenses, such as her clothing and new appliances and services.

It's been a financial strain for both of us which I think surprises your mother and shocks me, because I make money very easily and have done well ever since I finished my medical training. I am not accustomed to *having* to be careful, though for most of my life I have been.

So here I lie, early in the morning, feeling weak, lonely and isolated, wondering and worrying about money, about chores, about relationships and, of course, trying to imagine solutions and scenarios to everything.

Your life, I assure you, if nothing else, will never be dull.

Tom courted women in college, enjoyed their companionship and was not intimidated by them. Some fell in love with him. Taffy Van Dyke entered Springfield in the fall of 1958, just as Tom was starting his senior year. More than thirty years later, she still remembered vividly her first glimpse of him.

"Tom was standing talking with some friends," Taffy recalled. "He was dressed in his white gymnastics outfit, and I remember being extremely impressed with him. He was tall, good-looking, had an air of confidence about him, an air of very quiet leadership. I remember thinking, *This is the kind of young man I've really got to get to know.*"

Taffy greeted Tom every time she saw him on campus, and he responded, and soon they were chatting occasionally, then frequently. "We never really went out on what could be termed a date," Taffy said, "which disappointed me. But we did a lot of things together. We went to movies and would walk together after the movies and talk.

"By Christmastime, I was totally and completely in love with this man. I don't know whether he knew it or not, but everybody else on campus knew it. His gymnastics teammates knew it. Everybody in the dorm knew. During Christmas vacation I dragged my mother to five or six exhibitions by the gymnastics team in the New York/New Jersey area, and we'd always sit in the front row, and if Tom just looked my way and smiled, he made it all worthwhile.

"The friendship progressed. My love for him deepened, and I was only eighteen at the time, but I tried everything I could think of as a nice young, innocent girl to make him attracted to me. Nothing worked, and I really didn't know why. I thought about it a lot, and I didn't really think I was unattractive, but it certainly made me wonder.

"Then, in the late winter or early spring, Tom and I went to a movie and we were walking back across the practice field at Springfield, and it was dark, and he asked if I'd like to go to his apartment, he had some things he wanted to show me. And I was thrilled.

"I don't remember too much about the apartment because it was pretty dark. He turned on one light, and I just saw the one room where he had his desk and a filing cabinet. And he went into the cabinet and brought out pictures of Don Marshman and articles written about him and started talking about Don.

"And I didn't say much because it wasn't my position to say anything. I just listened. And then as he talked about it, he started to say something to me, and I remember thinking at the time, *Okay, this is it, he's going to tell me that he's gay.*

"I'd thought about that possibility other times, and I'd always pushed it to the back of my mind. I'd say, 'No, Taffy, you're being silly. He doesn't give any indication of being gay. He doesn't have any of the characteristics of a gay person.' Of course, I didn't know much about gay people at that time. I still don't.

"In his apartment, he started to say something to me, and I thought, *Okay, here it comes,* and then he stopped abruptly and changed the subject to something else. And I know now, and I think I knew then, that he came that close to confiding in me."

Almost thirty years later, Taffy wrote a letter to Tom.

May 1, 1987

Dear Tom:

As I began writing you last evening, it occurred to me that very likely you had been a more significant person in my life than I in yours, and it was very possible that—at worst—you might not even remember me. But whether you do or don't really is beside the point. I feel compelled to write you anyway because you were so very important to me!

Thoughts of you have been with me off and on over the past thirty years, sometimes brought on by seeing a mention of you in a magazine or a newspaper, sometimes for no particular reason at all. Now, after seeing you on *20/20*, I think of you again, this time with much sadness, but still with great admiration and pride.

You have changed little over the years, but accomplished much—a lot of which you have the right to be very proud of, if you were a prideful sort of person.

Thirty years ago (doesn't seem possible!) during my freshman year and your senior year at Springfield College, you were my best and closest friend, and I loved you dearly! Today I would like to be your friend again.

I wrote you after your superb performance in the 1968 Olympics. I have no idea if the letter ever reached you, but I wrote because I wanted you to have my congratulations and to know that we were watching the Games—and you—with great interest, excitement and pride.

That year of friendship you gave me thirty years ago has always been extremely important to me—you were a tremendous influence on me (of course, if you remember, I was also *completely* in love with you—in fact, so much so that of all the young men I saw or dated, you were the only one my husband Don was ever jealous of!).

That year we were always able to talk about anything and everything. Well, almost . . . How I wish you had been able to confide in me your emotional and physical leanings. I would have understood and I would have remained supportive as your friend. *Plus*, it would have helped me. I spent a lot of years wondering what was wrong with me that you couldn't find me attractive. I didn't find out until the article in *People* magazine that I really was OK.

I admire the wonderful things you've accomplished in your life. I am devastated, for you and all the people who love you, which includes me, that you are now suffering with such a monstrous illness. I wish you *well*, I pray you will beat it and spend many more years with the people you love. And I offer you a friendship of long ago, renewed. I know you have many wonderful, supportive friends to help you through this devastating time—I just want you to know I'm one of them.

I will be visiting my family (my sister lives in Del Mar, and my mother in La Jolla) sometime in August. It would please me greatly to see you again.

God bless you.

With friendship and love,
Taffy (Van Dyke) Bruce

Dear Taffy:

Do I remember you? Dear sweet friend, I remember everything about you and me. What a wonderful letter. It made me weep.

I'm sorry the circumstances that exist for me are the reason for our correspondence, but that is the way things are, and I have no trouble accepting them.

My one regret is that I caused you pain over my true nature. In retrospect, I would have been quite comfortable confiding in you, but it was the fifties and I just hid my own pain. Thank you for making my world a less lonely place. I loved you, too.

I'm happy these days. It's as though I'm going ninety miles an hour to get more in before I go.

Thanks again, friend. I always liked being seen with you on campus.

Oh, the fifties! Weren't they bad?

Love,
Tom

Tom died before Taffy had a chance to visit him.

August 29, 1983 (Same morning)

I am not sleeping well. Trying to adjust to being home again after those nightmarish days and nights in the hospital—the pain, the noise, the fear, the vulnerability and dependence— they all run against the one thing that is most important in my life: Freedom!

My dear child, I anticipate with joy the opportunity to share so much with you over the years. But it is probably essential that I tell you my thoughts and my actions and my dreams as I think of them. It will be many years before we will have deep and meaningful conversations.

My life has been an extremely busy one, exciting and rewarding. You will hear from many people that I have had a very successful life and I would imagine they would mean that both financially and socially. To that, I would say, "Yes," but it never occurred to me that life would *not* be that way, and so I don't attach as much importance to money and stature as others do. I have always felt that one's rewards were commensurate with the amount of effort that goes into creating something. This, I believe, is still generally true.

But if I were to characterize my own life, I would have to say that one of my chief motives in doing whatever I happened to be doing was a sense of adventure.

From the time I was old enough to think, I knew I wanted to experience as much as the world would permit me. I didn't feel any arbitrary restraints on fulfilling that desire.

When Tom was a senior at Springfield, he resolved a situation that had been troubling him for a number of years. He made up his mind to change his name legally from Flubacher to Waddell. Gene and Hazel Waddell eagerly adopted him.

"It was one of the most difficult things I've ever done," Tom said. "It hurt my father terribly. When I told him I was going to change my name, he said, 'If you do, you are no longer my son.' He was crying. I'll never forget his face. Then he went into his bedroom and closed the door, and I could have put a bullet through my head, I felt so bad."

Tom justified his decision by thinking of how much he felt he owed the Waddells. "I told myself I'm changing my name for two people who have done wonderful things for me," he said. "The Waddells awakened me, nurtured me. They wanted a child very much. They wanted to be able to say, 'This is our son, Tom Waddell.' "

But Tom recognized that his motives were not entirely unselfish. "I didn't like having a strange name, a funny name. People are affected by their names. People with strange names are often strange."

So Flubacher became Waddell, another of Tom's attempts, he said, "to fit in."

August 31, 1983

Here you are!

You are so beautiful!

It is now five a.m., and you are just over one hour old.

I am going home to call all the people on the East Coast who are waiting to hear about you—then a few hours' sleep.

I'll call:

Enge

Grandma Marion

Grandpa Elmer

Gene and Hazel Waddell

Goodnight, my dear, sweet, beautiful child, I am so glad to meet you face to face at last.

It is now four p.m. How about a re-cap?

Yesterday, Zohn, Eric, Roger and I went to one of the baseball parks to watch Mom's Artemis team play a game. We were to meet her there.

We arrived and Mom wasn't there. I saw some of the team members and one of them looked at me in shock. She said, "What are you doing *here*?" When I told her I had come to watch the game, she told me Sara had been admitted to hospital and was expected to deliver "tonight."

I rushed home and called.

Mom was in the hospital all right, being attended by Chris and Lindy [McKnight, a former lover]. I made plans to arrive about ten p.m. Mom's (and your) water bag broke about 4:30 in the afternoon and when Mom got to the hospital, she was about three cm. dilated and having regular contractions.

I did arrive about ten and joined Chris and Lindy in coaching Mom through the breathing exercises we had learned. Mom was doing very well, considering that she not only had to contend with your incipient arrival, but also with the three of us who were doting over her.

Things went smoothly until Mom was about five or six cm. and having really painful contractions. It was advised that she have a pain shot, which she accepted, but it had no effect on her pain. At about midnight, Mom was in such pain that she requested an epidural which would relieve the pain while not causing any risk to you.

Mom had to wait for 500 cc. of fluid to enter a vein in her arm before she could have the epidural. She struggled through another twenty minutes and then the epidural was put in place. Shortly thereafter Mom had almost no more pain and she began to feel happy and humorous again.

At about three this morning, Mom began pushing and we got our first glimpse of your head, just a little spot of hair.

With all of us coaching, Mom was able to push your head out at 3:50 a.m., and all of your beautiful self was officially BORN at 3:55 a.m.

The doctor clamped the umbilical cord and handed me the scissors to cut it.

You were suddenly on your own! I lifted you first and dried your head off and then placed you on Mom's breast.

All of us were ecstatic! What a joyous moment. At last we could welcome Jessica Waddell Lewinstein into the world.

I ran out to break the news and everyone got very excited. I even ran up to the fifth floor to tell the nurses and some of the patients I had gotten to know just two days earlier when I was being treated for my kidney stone.

Then I went home, and Chris stayed with Mom because Mom seemed to want it that way.

Tom Waddell received his bachelor's degree from Springfield in the spring of 1959, but he wasn't quite qualified to apply to medical school. To fulfill his premed requirements, to enable himself to carry on Don Marshman's, dream and become a doctor, he still had to study German and analytic chemistry.

But first he needed a summer job, and when a couple of his friends told him they were going to spend the summer as counselors at a place called Camp To-Ho-Ne in western Massachusetts, earning $500 or $600 apiece, Tom decided he would apply for a position, too.

The day after graduation, he drove to Great Barrington to be interviewed by the owner of Camp To-Ho-Ne, Peter Menaker, and his younger brother, Enge. The interview was brief, the verdict swift. "Hire him, hire him," Enge Menaker urged his brother.

Tom took the job, and his attitudes, his politics, his beliefs—his life—were never again the same.

Frederich Engels Menaker, named after Karl Marx's co-author of *The Communist Manifesto*, was called Enge, which rhymes with "range," and in the summer of 1959, when they met, he was 63, precisely three times as old as Tom Waddell. Enge was five feet two, perhaps five three if he stretched, fully a foot shorter than Tom. And while Enge was an avowed communist, who had successfully shifted his allegiance from Stalin to Khrushchev, Tom considered himself an Eisenhower Republican.

Enge became Tom's mentor and his lover, and they were a most unlikely pair.

Enge's parents were born in Russia, his mother in Odessa, his father in Vilna, and both fled from the czar and the Cossacks when they were young. They met in Paris and settled in the United States late in the nineteenth century. They had eight sons and named each of them, Enge informed Tom, after a prominent socialist.

In 1921 Peter Menaker, then thirty-one, a graduate of Michigan Agricultural College (which became Michigan State University), rented the site of a former girls' camp and opened Camp To-Ho-Ne for boys. The camp stood on the shores of Lake Buel in Great Barrington, in the foothills of the Berkshire Mountains, not far from the New York State border.

To-Ho-Ne started with two counselors and nineteen campers, and during the next decade, as Menaker acquired more acreage and built new bunks, the population swelled to a dozen counselors and more than 130 boys.

The camp offered swimming, hiking, woodwork, painting, nature study, theatrical productions, all the standard fare of summer camps. In 1926 Peter Menaker instituted an adult camp, a retreat for the families of the young campers; and in 1930 Enge Menaker and a former To-Ho-Ne counselor named Glen Memmen became the codirectors of the adult facility. They ran it together for thirty-three years, and they lived together for all those years.

Enge Menaker and Glen Memmen resided in an old farmhouse, known as The Farm, which had an almost mystical appeal to campers young and old.

Michael Zheutlin went to Camp To-Ho-Ne as a ten-year-old in 1966. "As a terribly homesick youngster," he recalled years later, "I was often at Enge's farm, eating breakfast, playing in the barn, and feeling a part of his extended family. I have vivid memories of pancakes on the porch, Ping-Pong in the garage, an overall feeling of warmth. The Farm can best be described as akin to Elrond's House in Tolkien's *Lord of the Rings*, known as the Last Homely House, a place where all good people were always welcome."

In the language of the Onondaga Indians, who once roamed the region, *To-Ho-Ne* meant "Here I Shall Camp." For Tom Waddell, it meant a new world to go with his new name.

September 20, 1983

For the first two days after you were born, many of us were in and out of the hospital, visiting you and Mom. She was feeling wonderful, and I could sense the immense bond that was going to develop between the two of you. Frankly, I felt excluded in some gnawing way as I saw Chris move in closer to Mom, and Mom seemed to be holding me at arm's length.

The joy turned to pain on the day you were to come home. Mom and I had been stockpiling some of the paraphernalia that the hospital had lying around; I think we would have taken the bed if it hadn't been so obvious. Your Mom then told me that Chris would take the two of you home and would stay overnight to help care for you. I felt deeply hurt and expressed my feelings to Mom, and I wept from the anguish over being shoved aside so ungracefully and insensitively. Lindy, too, was shocked, but things were left as planned even though Mom assured me she wanted my full participation as your father. Your Mom is truly a remarkable woman, but extremely headstrong and used to having things her own way. She can move me around any issue so easily because I know her to be so honest and forthright—but my heart was still aching.

The next two weeks were real horrors for me. Mom called all the shots and Chris was invited to be in a space that I was not. I became very resentful of Chris and I began to dislike her immensely. I saw her as rude and very much into control.

Mom and I had several discussions about all this, as did Lindy and Mom. Lindy and I both felt betrayed that we were being shoved aside.

Still, I had some hours with you and I would hold you and sing to you and play classical music—particularly Mozart—but I didn't feel like part of a family, and Chris was being very insensitive to the situation, as I believed Mom was. Truly, I felt so bad I didn't know what to do. Further, Mom would invite her friends over by the hordes, and yet I was discouraged from allowing my friends to do the same since it "violated" Mom's space. She was particularly hard on Zohn, as was Chris, when Zohn was being as loving and caring as could be.

It's complicated among Mom and Chris and Zohn. I don't know if they will ever work it out, though I trust the integrity of at least Mom and Zohn, and perhaps Chris will learn.

The big blow came when I began reading to you from a book I thought was your baby book. But it was Mom's diary. I should have closed it, but I read the page I had opened to. It was terrible, but I'm not sorry I read it. As wrong as I was, it was good that I read it.

I was holding you at the time, and I suddenly felt you were going to be a stranger to me. What I read convinced me that I was to have a very small role in your life.

I stared at you, and my dreams of raising a child of my own in equal partnership seemed to be gone.

I imagined you in your mid-teens and having you visit me. You were polite and beautiful, but at a distance from me. I imagined wanting to tell you how I felt about you when you first came into the world, how close I had planned to be to you and Mom, to share a sense of family. It all seemed to evaporate in front of me, and all I could see was this lovely woman who acknowledged me as her father, but didn't feel connected to me.

I planned, while I was lying there, to make a statement to Mom and then exit—for good. I felt betrayed and I felt like an ass. And I felt badly cheated.

Mom came home and I told her what I'd done. I apologized for reading what I did, but having done so told me that my worst fears were justified. I began going out the door when Mom called me and asked me to sit with her on the sofa. She excused Lindy from the room and then proceeded to put the entire entry into perspective and reassured me in the most forthright and loving manner so that I was swept off my feet once again by the love I felt for her.

I love Mom. She is beautiful not only in appearance, but in her character, which affects everyone the same way. She will be a great force in your life, and her strength may intimidate you, but that is fine as long as you learn from it. If you can acquire her strength, then none of us need ever fear for you.

The youngsters at Camp To-Ho-Ne were, for the most part, the well-educated children of New York Jewish socialists and liberals, and Tom Waddell's job, as a hired Gentile jock, was to teach them to flex their muscles as well as their minds. They were going to be writers and artists and composers, and he taught them to run and jump.

Tom became an icon to many of them and was placed on a pedestal, along with Norman Mailer and Leonard Bernstein and their other idols. "To say that at forty I have had only one hero in my life would be true," a man named Marc Krulewitz wrote to Tom a quarter of a century after his camp days. "To say that I have never bragged about knowing anyone except you would also be true. When I compounded my arm in high-school pole-vaulting and I was being wheeled into surgery, I thought of you. When I ran the 440, I could—I can still—hear you say, 'Relax on the back stretch and sort of ride on your hips.' And even a month ago, I was showing my nine-year-old daughter how to hurdle a saw horse and I could hear you say, 'Look for the imaginary box to step through.' Your sense of humor, your sense of strength, your caring nature have given me the ability to be free, to live free, to think free, not to be a quitter, or give up."

Of course, Tom learned from the children, from their families and, mostly, from Enge. Enge Menaker mesmerized people. He could speak several languages, play the guitar and the accordion, and call square dances in Spanish as comfortably as in English. He was a journalist by trade, a reporter and an editor. He had put in a stint in Washington, working side by side with a young newspaperman named Drew Pearson, who became an influential political columnist.

When the Spanish Civil War erupted during the mid-1930s, Enge made his way to the south of France to publish a magazine that echoed the Soviet Union's support of the Spanish loyalists. He struck up acquaintances with Ernest Hemingway and F. Scott Fitzgerald, and after the Civil War he helped Spaniards fleeing the Franco regime to relocate in France and in Mexico. In later years, when he visited Mexico, people poured out of little villages to greet and embrace him, to thank him for his compassion and his kindnesses.

Enge's life was the stuff of fiction, and Daniel Menaker, a gifted writer, the son of Enge's youngest brother, crafted several short stories—most of which appeared in *The New Yorker*—about a fictional "Uncle Sol," a character unmistakably based on Uncle Enge. The stories were collected in a book called *The Old Left*.

"As the leaves outside began their colorful demise," Daniel Menaker wrote, "the people at Uncle Sol's would dance to his square-dance calling, listen to his stories, sing songs with him and tolerate his condemnation, good-natured back then, of their profligate materialism. . . .

"Sol was the most social of socialists, with his square-dance calling and his vast repertoire of party games and his romantic and companionable version of Marxism. The young people who thronged to his place in the Berkshires fell in love with it, and as they grew older and money modified their politics, many of them bought land and houses in the neighborhood. . . .

"That formidable nose . . . had steered him in so many risky and romantic directions over his ninety years—from the trenches in the Argonne to the bleak hills around Madrid, and from there to a sometimes even more frightening battle against the Red-baiters and crypto-Fascists in this country in the middle of the century. . . ."

A charming blend of fact and fiction, like Enge himself.

Tom couldn't believe how lucky he was to fall under Enge's spell. He suspected he was falling in love.

In the summer of 1959 Tom Waddell was still not totally secure in his instincts, still more than a little schizophrenic sexually. He loved Enge from a distance while he nurtured a closer relationship with a fellow To-Ho-Ne counselor and Springfield student named Bea Brown. Like Tom, Bea was raised a Catholic. "Which made it easier for us not to get physically involved," Tom recalled.

Bea was a beautiful young woman, Tom said, and like him, she found Enge irresistible. Sometimes when Tom and Bea made plans to go hiking or swimming, they invited Enge to join them and he would smile and say, "No, you young people go and enjoy yourselves." Enge encouraged them to be close. He was their friend, the counselors' counselor. He was no more Tom's lover, at that moment, than Bea was.

When Tom and Bea returned to Springfield in the fall of 1959, their relationship flourished. Tom sold his car so that he could buy Bea a diamond engagement ring. They were both seeking an escape from Catholicism, not so much from the physical restraints as from the mental ones. "We were both totally disenchanted," Tom said. "Every week we went to a different church, to try it out, to see if there was a viable alternative to Catholicism."

One Sunday Tom and Bea went to a service at the First Congregational Church of Springfield and settled into seats behind a little old woman who offered a running commentary throughout the service. "Fucking son of a bitch," she muttered. "Cocksucking motherfucker. Asshole prick."

Tom looked at Bea. Bea looked at Tom. Catholicism almost made a comeback.

After the service, several parishioners clustered around the young couple and apologized for the obscene interruptions. "Please, please, don't assume that's what our congregation is like," someone said. "She's sick."

The woman was suffering from Tourette's syndrome, a nervous disorder that is often marked by involuntary swearing. It had nothing to do with the ailing woman, but Tom began to lean perceptibly toward atheism. Just as he had already begun to lean toward acceptance of his own sexuality.

One afternoon in 1960—early in his second summer at Camp To-Ho-Ne and not long after his splendid showing in the national championships—Tom decided, after a long day spent cleaning up the camp, to go for a swim. He stripped off his clothes and dived into Lake Buel and swam for almost an hour, cooling himself, cleansing himself.

When he came ashore, Enge was standing by his clothes with a large towel. Enge wrapped the towel around Tom and said, "You look cold, you look tired. Why don't you go up to my room and take a nap and we'll fix you some supper?"

Tom accepted gratefully. *This man is just so sweet,* he thought. *I love this man.*

Tom followed Enge to the room Enge shared with Glen Memmen. He lay down on Glen's bed.

"You can stay here tonight if you want," Enge said.

After he fed Tom, Enge got into his own bed and he and Tom chatted, calling to each other for a while.

"Look, you don't have to shout across the room," Enge said. "Why don't you come over here and we can talk quietly?"

Tom crossed the room and lay down next to Enge. Their conversation continued softly, more gently.

"Would you be offended," Enge asked, "if I hugged you?"

"No," Tom said. "As a matter of fact, I'd like that."

"What we did that first night," Tom recalled more than a quarter of a century later, "was called the Princeton rub. We just held each other, and I said, 'Enge, I love you,' and he said, 'You know, boy, I think I love you, too.'

"And I felt whole."

Glen Memmen spent the night, Tom eventually learned, sleeping on a nearby balcony.

Memmen came from Minnesota. He met Enge Menaker at an opera during the 1920s, and they fell in love. Enge, at that time, was engaged to be married.

"Glen was reticent, passive, much quieter than Enge," Tom said. "He was exquisitely sensitive and very bright. Enge told me he really didn't understand his nature until he met Glen."

Tom was puzzled then and later, as were others, by Glen's easy acceptance of the bond between Enge and Tom. He pressed Enge for an explanation but never got a very satisfactory one. "We are the most important persons in each other's lives," Enge offered.

"They were mad about each other," Tom said.

The relationship between Enge Menaker and Glen Memmen lasted almost forty years, survived the Spanish Civil War and World War II, survived McCarthyism and homophobia, survived even Tom's arrival at The Farm. But it ended in 1963, when Glen died of cancer.

• • •

"Enge educated me," Tom said. "He made me feel special. He made me feel loved."

When Tom realized that he was in love with Enge, and Enge in love with him, he wanted to tell the world. "I wanted everyone to know that I had finally found the partner I was looking for," Tom said. "I wanted everyone to know how wonderful he was. I was so happy. I was so proud."

But Tom shared his secret with no one.

Enge was the first person to tell Tom that it was all right to be a homosexual, that he was not alone, that he was not bizarre. But Enge was a product of a different time, and he also warned Tom never to admit his homosexuality to anyone. "He was a bit Edwardian," Tom said. " 'You can do whatever you want, but don't scare the horses.' "

At The Farm, the subject of homosexuality was practically taboo. Even years later, members of Enge's family and good friends would concede, if pressed, that Enge was a communist but not that he was gay. They perpetuated a heterosexual myth, and so did Enge himself. He loved to flirt with women, tease them, escort them.

"*You* people may be homosexual," Enge told Tom on more than one occasion, "but I am not. I am a heterosexual."

"Enge was not handsome in any conventional way," Tom said. "He was old, he was wrinkled. But he had a smile that was devastating. I loved his face. I could never photograph him enough."

The idea that Tom and Enge might be lovers did not come easily to the people who knew both of them. "People knew that I loved Enge," Tom said, "but they didn't see it as a physical thing."

Sex was not, in fact, the essence of the relationship, but it was not ignored. "We didn't just jump in bed every time we saw each other," Tom said. "I mean, our sex life was good. We would go to bed at night and cuddle and kiss and caress, and we had our own rituals, but it wasn't a big thing. What we had was truly a marriage in every sense of the word."

The great difference in their ages did not faze Tom; if anything, the gap drew him to Enge. "I've always loved getting older," Tom said. "I've always loved people in their forties. I thought, *Gee, there's something magical about that age.* Just the sound of the word *forty* was sexual to me. I was never interested in 'beautiful young men.' "

Later in his life Tom was irritated by the ageism he encountered in the gay community. "It's far worse than it is in the dominant culture," he said. "The gay culture is such a youth-oriented culture."

Until AIDS. AIDS took the aging and the young.

September 26, 1983

Just over three weeks old. I spend a good deal of time with you. Mom needs to tend to Artemis and other community projects and she needs time to play. We are good around each other lately, trading stories about our experiences with you.

Tonight Mom and I took you to a softball game. Her "D" team was playing (and won). I looked after you, feeding you, keeping you warm, humming to you and changing you. You sure are a voracious eater, and your BM's are commensurate with your intake. Next week you and Mom and I and Grandma Helen and Grandpa Jack [Sara's mother and stepfather] will go to Lake Tahoe. We have the home of a friend of mine for a few days and plan to enjoy ourselves while you become acquainted with Grandma and Grandpa, who have not seen you yet.

Last night Zohn and I spent the evening with you. We played Scrabble and you were an angel.

After Tom and Dick Wotruba competed in the 1960 U.S. decathlon championship—Tom's trip to the meet in Eugene, Oregon, which also served as the Olympic trials, was financed by the Wyckoff, New Jersey, Lion's Club—he was ready to start real life at medical school.

Someone had told Tom that when he interviewed for med school he should tell the interviewer, "I want to help people, and I hate money." For Tom, this would have been a half truth. "I didn't hate the money by any means," he said. "But I wanted to be involved in people's health in a very intimate way."

He was accepted at the New Jersey College of Medicine, a division of Seton Hall University.

For a few months Tom managed to juggle his studies, his love affair with Enge, and his engagement to Bea Brown. The engagement was announced in a New Jersey newspaper—**THOMAS WADDELL TO WED NEW TEACHER**—although the paper noted that no date had been set for the wedding. Bea taught science at Ramapo High School and lived with Gene and Hazel Waddell during Tom's first year in medical school.

Tom could not bring himself to tell Bea he was gay. "I used to think that maybe if I married her, I'd get over it," he said. But unlike many gay men he later knew in San Francisco, who chose to be husbands and fathers and remained closeted for decades, Tom decided that he couldn't deceive himself. "My feelings were stronger than ever," he said. "I thought, *I can't submerge these feelings for the rest of my life. I'll go crazy.*"

He went home one weekend and told his fiancée, "Bea, I'm not in love with you. I love you, but I'm not in love with you. And I don't think our marriage would work." He was being honest, though only up to a point.

Bea was surprised and hurt. She returned Tom's ring, and although she continued to live with the Waddells for the rest of the school year, she avoided Tom. He stayed away from the house for months. He felt, he said, "like a rat." When the school year ended, Bea moved away. Tom was saddened, disappointed with himself for inflicting pain, yet relieved that he would not have to live the lie of a heterosexual marriage.

Bea Brown had no such consolation. She disappeared from Tom's life, did not communicate with him for more than twenty years, not until she, like so many others whose lives he had touched, wrote to him after learning that he was dying of AIDS.

Tom's love for Enge blossomed. If he had six hours of free time at medical school, he would drive for two and a half hours to see Enge for an hour, then drive back to school.

Not everyone loved Enge quite so wholeheartedly. Some found him to be demagogic, at times mean-spirited, and certainly hypocritical about his sexuality, hiding as he did behind a smoke screen of female friends. Enge would needle his wealthier Jewish friends with anti-Semitic, antimaterialistic remarks. On some subjects, like Russia, he could not tolerate debate. To Enge, communism was a religion, the Soviet Union its shrine.

And yet, despite his blind spots and flaws, Enge reigned as the guru of To-Ho-Ne, the heart of an intellectual cult. Joseph Heller, the author of *Catch-22*, one of the great American novels of the twentieth century, spent summers at To-Ho-Ne. So did William Schuman, who became the president of Lincoln Center, the cultural core of Manhattan.

People vied to be close to Enge, to earn his approval. "If

Enge liked you," said Suellen Manning, whom Tom introduced to The Farm, "it made you feel like you were an okay
person, not so dumb, not so ugly. Whatever it was that was
your own personal insecurity, it wasn't there anymore. He
made you feel secure about yourself."

"You had to prove your mettle to become part of the inner
circle," said Tom. He was the golden boy, said Connie
Sussman, who, with her husband, Jack, was among the regulars at The Farm. "He was everybody's favorite." And Tom was
like a sponge, absorbing everything he could about politics and
dance and music and literature. He swung from Eisenhower
Republican to Enge Radical.

Enge could coerce college presidents and famous authors
into helping with the dishes and enjoying every moment. They
would cheerfully listen to whatever he had to say, even if,
sometimes, they didn't believe a word of it.

At the beginning, Tom believed everything Enge said and
accepted his word as gospel. He may have been gullible, but
he was surely growing.

Still, Tom worried about his sexuality. Although he was in love
with Enge, he continued to cultivate relationships with
women. He never talked about homosexuality with the women
he dated. If a woman asked him whether he had any homosexual feelings, he shivered inwardly.

"Why do you ask that?" he would respond. "Did I do
something?"

Again, he wrote of himself as a fictional character, as
"Jerry" in a journal entry.

Jerry needs to be thought of as a strong masculine person. That's the image he puts his energy into . . . He's
even smart enough to avoid the trap of protesting if
someone should question his masculinity . . . Once,

someone, in a half-serious tone, accused Jerry of being "a muscle queen." Jerry despised the idea that anyone would refer to him as any kind of queen—but he deflected the "insult" by saying, "Ah, yes, the muscle queen! She ruled England in the mid-1600s—noted for her proclivity for mollusks, thought of them as aphrodisiacs. Yes, very attractive person, she!"

Humor was one of the weapons Tom used. The occasional heterosexual encounter was another. He pursued one woman, he said, "like a dog in heat," and finally, ever the athlete, had sex with her on a playing field at Smith College in Massachusetts. "I was panting the whole time," Tom remembered. "When it was over, I thought, *Gee, I'm okay.* Then I thought, *No, I'm really not.*

Tom's first couple of years of medical school were difficult, academically and logistically. He spent as many weekends as he could at The Farm, and in between he wrote a stream of letters to Enge. When Enge asked Tom why he wrote to him so often, Tom answered sarcastically, "Yes, who the hell are you to expect someone to take the time to write to you every day? You're only the source of all my enthusiasm, my optimism; you're only the target of all my deepest emotions; you're only the difference between a small, ignorant existence and a broad, wonderful life."

Medical school meant long hours of class and lab work, followed by longer hours of study. Survival demanded commitment, sacrifice, and a touch of black humor. Tom never forgot one class in which he and a group of fellow students studied a cadaver that had a noticeably large penis. As they were dissecting the body, Tom flipped the penis out of the way. It landed on a female student's hand, and she flipped it back. For several minutes, the two of them volleyed the penis back and forth until the woman marched out of the classroom, obviously offended. The next day, when the class arrived, the penis was standing at attention. The young woman had tied a string around the organ and rigged it to an overhead pipe.

Although medical school and Enge consumed much of his energy, Tom still felt a need to make time for athletics. He trained as a member of the prestigious New York Athletic Club team in 1961 and 1962; and in the national indoor championships in 1962, he finished third in the high jump, with a leap of six feet four inches.

His performance was good enough to earn him an invitation from the Amateur Athletic Union and the U.S. State Department to tour Africa with a track-and-field team, under the auspices of President John F. Kennedy's cultural-exchange program. He took a leave of absence from medical school and joined sprinters Calvin Barnes and Brooks Johnson, miler Pete Close, and pole vaulter Henry Wadsworth, all world-class athletes, on a tour through Ethiopia, Libya, Sudan, Morocco, Ghana, Tunisia, and Egypt. At each stop, the athletes demonstrated their ability by competing against local stars, then conducted seminars on track-and-field technique.

The two-month trip—in May and June of 1962—gave Tom his first taste of international travel, and he was hooked. He decided he wanted to go everywhere, see everything, meet everybody. He hardly ever turned down an opportunity to travel, and he boasted that, of all his trips around the globe, there was only one that he paid for himself.

On his maiden journey he swam in the Red Sea, walked the tortuous streets of ancient cities, witnessed squalid Third World poverty, and attended extravagant embassy parties at which he feasted on stories of despots and coups. He shopped in souks and ate couscous. He visited Fez and Rabat, Tripoli and Benghazi.

Tom mingled with the poor and the powerful, befriending a street boy named Majid in Morocco and encountering Emperor Haile Selassie in Ethiopia. He offered medical treatment to Majid's mother and gave the poor family food and money. Majid begged Tom to bring him back to America, but Tom had neither the funds nor the clout to do this. He was dismayed by the lack of medicine in Morocco; his interest in tropical medicine was sparked at that time. Tom was impressed by Haile Selassie, the Lion of Judah, but even more impressed by another Ethiopian, Abebe Bikila, the reigning Olympic marathon champion.

For most of the trip Tom roomed with Brooks Johnson, a fortuitous match. Johnson was only a few years out of Tufts University, and he was, like Tom, a man of remarkably varied skills and interests. He was a writer, an actor, and a social activist (he once worked with the socialist Saul Alinsky in Chicago) before deciding to concentrate on coaching track and field. Eventually he became the head coach at Stanford University, then coach of the U.S. women's team in the 1984 Olympic Games.

Johnson was a perceptive young man. "I could tell from the start that there was a struggle going on within Tom," he recalled. "He had feelings that he didn't quite know how to handle. He was a contradiction—what he looked like, what he acted like. A dichotomy—his gentleness and his drive to be supermacho. He even chose the most macho of events—the decathlon."

Waddell and Johnson, a black man, spent hours discussing politics, poverty, and prejudice, not quite the usual fare for athletes on an overseas junket. "He was attracted to less-advantaged people," Johnson theorized, "because they were much more accepting, much more open, much more tolerant. They weren't threatening. All that mattered was how good a person you were."

"I liked Brooks," Tom said, "and he could feel it. He could

sense the total lack of judgment about his color. He was just a person who happened to be black, and we became very good friends. He was very funny. We could talk about just about anything."

Their paths would cross many times, at the Olympic Games in Mexico in 1968, when they both lived in Washington, and also in the Bay Area. "He never came right out and told me of his sexual preference," Johnson said. "He didn't trust me enough to tell me, but he hinted at it." Brooks watched Tom progress from "brutal repression" to "emancipation."

Shortly before Jessica was born, Tom called Brooks at Stanford. "He was yelling, 'I'm going to have a baby, I'm going to have a baby,'" Johnson said. "Not, 'I'm going to be a father,' but, 'I'm going to have a baby.' I think there was a part of him that really felt he was going to have the baby.

"When we first met, he knew even then that he was going to do something special. He just wasn't sure what it was. His child is his legacy."

Johnson was as articulate as any of the crowd at The Farm, and his tongue was just as sharp. "Want to know the two most overrated races in the Olympics?" Brooks Johnson liked to say. "The marathon—and the white."

Tom, thanks to Enge's influence, considered himself at the time a Marxist, but the trip to Africa tempered his radicalism. He was now willing to concede that the United States might not be the worst country in the world: "It might even be the best," he wrote to Enge. The U.S., he reported, "has done some wonderful things here."

Still, Tom did witness examples of "Ugly Americanism": the chauvinism of the coach of the touring team, the bigotry of American servicemen, and the self-important, self-serving

air of U.S. diplomats. He was sufficiently embarrassed to apologize to several of his African hosts.

Then he returned to America and spent the rest of his
leave from medical school with Enge.

September 28, 1983

I have put together a new board of directors to take charge
of Gay Games II. Last night we had our first business
meeting and I legally transferred the power of the corporation to a new president. Mom and Chris and a few other
friends all sit on the board. I am hoping, after two years
of devoting my time, energy and money to the project, to
have a salaried position as executive director. I am also considering beginning a new medical practice right here on
Albion.

Today I spent seven hours with you—it was delightful.
You are probably still unaware of me—though all I have read
suggests that you may be identifying individuals. You stared
at me while I sang to you and talked to you and fed you.
Most of all I like changing your diapers and cleaning and
drying your bottom. You have begun to associate that activity with comfort and since I think I do it quite well, it gives
me pleasure to make you warm and dry again.

I love you very much.

Mom and I are beginning to have fun with you and it
makes us even closer. I love Mom very much, too. My life is
strange (it's always been strange!), but I feel a lovely calm
these days, and a great deal of that comes from being with
you and Mom—and watching you grow.

You are four weeks old today.

Grandpa (my father) sent a check for $50 for you. I will
put it into a special account that will be exclusively yours and

when you are eighteen, I will turn it over to you to do with it whatever you wish.

Eric and Roger and Zohn all ask about you every day.

I once asked Tom Waddell if he had ever failed at anything, and he thought for a while and then quietly replied, "No."

He almost failed at medical school. He wasn't exactly focused on medicine. "I was so politically involved in the sixties," he explained. "I was just in a rage about the Vietnam War. It distracted me from medicine."

While he was in school he worked for the Central Committee for Conscientious Objectors, and ran a clinic for the militant Black Panthers. For his efforts, he became known as Tommie the Commie, a lonely radical at a strict and conservative Catholic school. "I was very disenchanted with med school," he said. "I wanted to get through all the academic stuff and get out and treat people. It was a real struggle."

He all but gave up athletic competition, rarely even finding time to work out. Still, he graduated with an M.D. degree in the spring of 1965 and was accepted as an intern at Beth El Hospital in Brooklyn. He was to report in July.

Before Tom began his internship, he took his second overseas trip, this one to Europe, funded by friends from The Farm. He was scheduled to travel with Enge and a mutual friend named Jose, but Jose was killed in an automobile accident just days before the scheduled start of the trip. This loss, following so closely on the death of Glen Memmen two years earlier, devastated Enge. "There's little left to the man, and I think I am holding that little bit together," Tom wrote in a diary. "My love could not be greater, but will it be enough?"

Enge was so distraught he decided at the last moment not to go to Europe. Tom went alone, and for three weeks he toured Italy, Switzerland, France, and England. Although he missed Enge terribly ("I know this sounds silly, but I miss your rump touching mine as we sleep," he wrote) and was haunted by the death of Jose at every turn, he managed to enjoy the trip. He flirted with Italian women but did not have great difficulty rejecting the proposition of a middle-aged prostitute in Florence at one in the morning. "Too tired," Tom explained, lying to his journal.

When he returned from Europe he found a sad, empty Enge. The love of his life seemed old and depressed. Tom felt Enge had lost "all his talents and abilities." He longed for "the Enge of old."

In July Tom began his internship at Beth El Hospital, which was renamed Brookdale Hospital the same year. He moved into an apartment in Manhattan.

Throughout the stifling summer he endured the crushing duties of medical internship, drained by twenty-four-hour shifts in the emergency room, during which he'd often see more than 200 patients, and put stitches in most of them. Tom had always had an uncommonly high pain threshold, but he found the fatigue to be agony.

It was not long before he experienced his first death as a doctor. One day he was talking to a patient, and the next day his "guts are sprawled all over a table." He recoiled at the thought of his power, the doctor's "godlike activities." Yet he grew more confident of his abilities and more comfortable around patients. Tom Waddell's bedside manner, like his athletic skills, never needed much formal training. He was a natural.

The summer of 1965 was an explosive time in the civil-rights movement, a summer of tension and action and violence: Three civil-rights volunteers, two of them from New York, one a local black, were murdered in Mississippi. Tom was angry and frustrated. He had a three-week vacation coming up in the fall, and he decided to do whatever he could to help. He contacted a group called the Medical Committee for

Human Rights and volunteered his services. The committee agreed to cover his room and board, and dispatched him to Selma, Alabama, to provide medical care for local blacks and civil-rights volunteers. He was also to give lectures on public health in towns throughout the region.

He arrived in Selma on October 23, expecting utter chaos. Instead, he found "an Uncle Remus world filled with charming whites and charming blacks." His clinic was a small room with sleeping bags on the floor and no furniture. There wasn't a great deal to do, except experience the place and the time. Tom hung out with a small black boy who liked to spend time at the clinic; the two of them would pass warm fall evenings throwing stones at pecan trees and collecting bags and bags of the ripe nuts.

The volunteers were living in a ramshackle hut where Tom met a young black woman named Martha, who opened up to him the world of southern blacks. He visited their homes, drank in their bars, sang in their churches on Friday nights and Sunday mornings. On occasion he was invited to address a congregation, to share his feelings.

One night he met Stokely Carmichael, the prickly leader of SNCC, the Student Nonviolent Coordinating Committee. Carmichael was suspicious of outsiders, particularly of whites. "What you want, whitey?" Stokely demanded of Tom.

"I'm here to help."

"We don't need your help, whitey," Carmichael said.

"No," Tom said, "I think you do. I think you need all the help you can get."

"Who the hell is this guy?" Stokely Carmichael snapped.

Tom's friend Martha stepped in. "Oh, Stokely," she said. "Cut it out."

Later in his stay Tom was assigned to travel to a middle-of-nowhere town called Geez Bend to lecture on public health.

He found the town and enjoyed the talk. The people were warm and genuinely interested in what he had to say about nutrition, sexually transmitted diseases, and other health issues.

Then, as he was driving back to Selma after the lecture, he was pulled over by the local police—a frightening experience for any civil-rights worker, especially a northerner. Although he was driving at a legal speed, the cops dragged him out, shoved him against his car, and banged his head on the hood. They frisked him, peppered him with questions. Who are you? Where are you? What are you doing here? Where have you been, boy? And with whom?

"We know all about you," one of the officers told Tom, then charged him with reckless driving and ordered him to jail.

"I couldn't agree with you more," Tom responded.

"What?" said the cop.

"Nothing, nothing," Tom said. He was tempted to deliver a lecture on racism and human rights, but with the murder of the civil-rights workers still fresh news, even he knew enough not to be too much of a smartass.

The police placed Tom in a small cell, and as he sat there, wondering what would happen next, the sheriff walked in. The sheriff was Jim Clark, who was famous, or infamous, for his resistance to the march from Selma to Montgomery, the massive civil-rights demonstration that had taken place only a few months earlier.

Clark told Tom Waddell to look out the window of his cell. "Boy, you see that land?" the sheriff asked. "That's my daddy's land. My granddaddy and my great-granddaddy all lived here. We always been peaceful." He launched into a long story about how he and his family always took care of the land, always took care of the people who worked the land, the Negroes, which was a difficult word for a southern sheriff to pronounce properly.

"Why's a nice boy like you down here stirring up trouble?" Clark wanted to know. "A fine man like you, rabble-rousin'? I don't understand it. Don't you know better?"

Tom said nothing. Clark turned and smacked him across the head. "You better listen to me, boy," he suggested.

Tom, aware he might be pistol-whipped, or worse, wisely said nothing.

The sheriff handed him a book. "You read this, boy," Clark said. "I'm leavin' your light on all night, and I'm gonna ask you some questions about it in the morning."

The book was called *Race, Heredity and Civilization*, and was written by a professor from North Carolina. Its thesis was predictable: Blacks are inferior to whites historically, genetically, socially, culturally, every way.

Tom stayed up all night reading the book and was ready, even eager, to debate the sheriff in the morning. But Clark never showed up. Instead, a representative of the Medical Committee for Human Rights appeared and paid Tom's fine of $25, plus $24 for court costs. And he was allowed to leave.

He spent the next few days "being leisurely," in the local idiom, reflecting on his brief experiences in the South. The region, he felt, was in transition. Segregated waiting rooms and rest rooms in the hospitals shocked him, but Martha assured him that these were disappearing. He felt uncomfortable with revolutionary approaches to civil-rights problems; evolution seemed a more productive course. "I don't like the idea of simply demanding that people think a certain way," he said.

Then he returned to a year of residency at Montefiore Hospital in the Bronx. He took a job moonlighting in the New York prison system, working at Riker's Island in the bay near LaGuardia Airport and at The Tombs, the detention center in lower Manhattan. He found the prisons "demeaning and ugly and ferocious.

"Talk about pits, talk about lousy medicine, talk about snake pits and people who have no way out," he said. "Guys used to wrap razor blades in cardboard and then swallow them so when the cardboard was digested, the razors would cut up their intestines and they'd have to be sent to Bellevue Hospital. They'd do anything to get out of The Tombs."

Once Tom had to enter a cell jammed with twenty black inmates to administer Valium to a convulsing heroin addict. The other inmates encircled him, menacing, threatening, demanding. "Hey, whitey, save me some of that," one said. "I need it more than he does."

"But there's a certain camaraderie in there, too. They didn't want to see the guy convulsing anymore. They let me in. They let me give him the Valium."

Still, Tom admitted, he was terrified. He worked as fast as he could because the guards seemed even more frightened than he was, and he wasn't sure they would be willing or able to come to his rescue if the inmates decided they had to have his hypodermic needle.

October 8, 1983

Well, we took you on your first long-distance ride—to Lake Tahoe—Mom, you and I, Grandma Helen and Grandpa Jack. It was pleasant for me because I had fun being with all of you. It was a different kind of fun—that I could only characterize as "family fun." Your Mom and I were treated like a young married couple. It was fine—just another occasion to be proud and playful. We took turns being with you—and the others would go play. I took Grandma and Grandpa to my two favorite places up there—Fallen Leaf Bay and Emerald Bay. They were thrilled, and I was pleased.

My private time with you was wonderful though I did become exasperated a few times when you kept crying in spite of all my efforts to find a reason, and when you shit three times in ten minutes while I was feeding you.

Mom and I were good friends throughout and had lots of pleasure in our company.

Apparently, Mom and Grandma had a serious argument regarding your care and Mom's adequacy as a mother. When I called the morning after we returned, Grandma and Grandpa had already departed at 5:30 in the morning. Whoops! I don't know what happened and didn't ask.

Your Mom and Zohn are not friends. Mom distrusts Zohn and Zohn feels hurt by Mom. They are both wonderful and fair people, but I have discovered that one cannot make two people be friends. Sometimes the chemistry is simply not in favor of it. I hope in this case that the chemistry can be altered.

Zohn and Mom had lunch together last week, and Zohn tried to explain himself to Mom. It wasn't satisfactory.

Zohn is accepting the notion that he will not be important to your childhood, but he is mistaken. He says he will be there and when you can meet as friends, it will happen at its own time. I think that time is near, and I ask him to be patient.

I have been desperate to begin making some money, and I've wanted to do it while working on Gay Games II.

In the spring of 1966, to his own shock and dismay, Tom Waddell, physician and antiwar radical, received an invitation to join the United States Army. It was an offer he couldn't refuse, not legally. "What will everyone think, me going into the army?" he wrote to Enge. "How embarrassing! How wrong!"

Tom's military career, strangely, turned out just fine. Instead of embarrassing himself, he distinguished himself, not in combat but as a member of the United States Olympic team.

•   •   •

On August 15, 1966, Tom Waddell and a friend named Steve Schwartz, who was also an intern at Brookdale, joined 2,000 other young doctors for basic training at the elaborate Fort Sam Houston military complex in Texas.

Their regimen was not quite so arduous as, say, infantry training. Each of the young doctors was first given $500 for spending money and a list of items to purchase, including uniforms. They were also provided with an allowance to cover their meals. Fresh from several stressful and sleepless months as interns, the doctors did not waste their money on food. "We broke up the town," Tom said. "Guys were drunk from seven in the morning till midnight."

They discovered that their base was a khaki country club offering the best food, the best golf course, the best swimming pool, and the best amenities tax dollars could buy. "And the minute we set foot in this country club," Tom said, "we were captains, and there were thousands of enlisted men saluting us all the time and kowtowing to us."

The required physical training was a breeze for Tom, but a sterner test for some of his fellow doctors, like Steve Schwartz, who were still recovering from the fatigue of internship. After six weeks of basic training, Tom and Steve volunteered for the army's preventive-medicine school, which meant ten weeks more of training at Fort Sam Houston. They would, however, have enough free time to travel throughout Texas and into Mexico.

But the specter of Vietnam was becoming more visible.

In the fall, Captain Schwartz was assigned to the Ninth Infantry Division. He received orders to report to Vietnam in November. "I've never seen anybody so scared in my life," said Tom, who was more fortunate. He was assigned to the 82nd Airborne Division at Fort Benning, Georgia, as a preventive-medicine officer, primarily to prevent venereal diseases.

Tom volunteered for extra training as a paratrooper.

"When they asked for volunteers," he explained, "my hand just shot out. I thought, *God, I want to jump out of a plane—just for the sheer fun of it.* I didn't care how hard I had to work. Could you imagine putting on a parachute and jumping out of a plane? I couldn't wait."

Of course Tom wanted to be a paratrooper—it was the most macho thing a soldier could do. The only hitch was that he was terrified of jumping from planes, but he was fascinated by his own fear. "I always love to do the things that scare me," he said. "I thought, *Wow, there's something I'm afraid of. All right, go after it. Go after it and get it out of the way.* It was always a magnet for me."

Tom confessed that he was afraid every time he jumped. Once, paralyzed by his fear as he perched on the strut of a helicopter—jumping from choppers was especially scary—he simply could not move. His instructor was very supportive. "He just put his foot up and pushed me off," Tom said. "I thought I was going to die."

He survived the jump, and jump school, which was at once the most exhilarating three weeks of his life and the most insane. "I saw enough craziness to last me a lifetime," Tom said. "The people involved were just nuts. They would have gone out without a parachute, I know they would have."

He jumped with one man who carried a gun, two knives and a hand grenade, and muttered, "I can't wait to get over there. Kill those fucking Cong! I just can't wait!"

"And he was the company chaplain," Tom said. "He was a Protestant minister. I thought, *Oh, God, we are in big trouble. There's something wrong here.*"

Tom also served with UDT soldiers, Underwater Demolition Team members, who spent their days training themselves into a frenzy and their nights drinking themselves into a stupor. Tom found himself jogging shirtless through freezing rain, flanked by soldiers chanting, "Kill the Cong! Kill the Cong!"

He even found himself chanting sometimes; it was a catchy tune.

"All the while I was thinking, *I can't believe I'm here*," Tom said. "*My family would kill me if they ever knew about this.*"

After jump school Tom turned to what he thought would be a less-hazardous diversion. He discovered that the army was offering a course in global medicine at Walter Reed Hospital outside Washington, D.C., a subject well suited to his credentials, experience, and interest. His application was approved, and he enrolled in February 1967.

Tom soon found there was a catch involved: Once he finished, he would be shipped to Vietnam. He immediately wrote to Colonel Bedford Berry, the army's chief of professional assignments.

I believe my intentions regarding future actions should be brought to your attention at this time. I have tried, in several "legitimate ways," to withdraw from the Global Medicine course since I discovered that a tour of Vietnam follows the course. I have been opposed, in conscience and on moral grounds, to the Vietnam war and our role in it for several years and I decided long before I entered the army that I would avoid serving there if possible and would refuse to go, and suffer the consequences, if there was no other alternative . . .

I had originally decided to finish the course, in hope of a change in the situation during the next six months. However, I think it would be dishonest and unfair to occupy that slot without first making known my convictions and thereby avoiding an unfortunate confrontation in July.

He was allowed to continue the course, but for the next six months he struggled with his decision. He wrote frequently to Steve Schwartz in Vietnam and reviewed the issue with him. "I'm already part of the war machine which is taking innocent lives," Tom noted. "Being THERE and directly contributing is a little too much for me to swallow. . . . As for those who love me and would suffer if I went to jail, those same people would suffer a great deal more if I went to Vietnam and got my stupid head shot off."

Clearly, there were limits to Tom's need to accept macho challenges.

Curiously, Enge Menaker thought Tom should go to Vietnam. Enge's influence was still powerful, and Tom later wrote to Schwartz that he had changed his mind, that he had decided to ship over. He began asking Steve questions: Have you had any contact with the Viet Cong? How do they regard physicians? How much latitude do you have for traveling alone?

But even Enge, usually so certain of himself, was conflicted. He, too, wrote to Schwartz about Tom's change of heart: "Personally, I am not sure how I feel about it, though I may have in a small way contributed to this turn of things. . . . The relief I feel is boundless though mixed with fury and frustration."

Disappointed by the stumbling efforts of the Johnson administration to pursue peace talks, and angered by rumors that the United States planned to escalate the war and invade North Vietnam, Tom soon changed his mind again. He would refuse to go. "I'm sure I would have plenty of company in jail," he wrote to Schwartz.

By late April of 1967, Tom had received his military assignment to Southeast Asia and had resolved not to go. He approached the American Civil Liberties Union to see if it would represent him if he were court-martialed. The ACLU responded favorably.

"Steve," Tom wrote, "I just can't go. I've been batting this thing around for a long time and listening to all kinds of advice. I've changed my mind many times and found no satisfaction. I concluded that I had to do what I think is right—and STICK TO IT. I have decided, and I am sticking to it. I'd rather go to jail than participate in the war.

"I've always been afraid of authority and I'm shitting in my pants now, but I'd feel a lot worse for many years if I change positions now to play it safe."

Tom was on good terms with his commanding officer, Colonel Joseph Cooch, whom he considered a friend and who considered him a surrogate son. He went to his CO's home and explained that unless he was reassigned—excused from duty in Vietnam—he would apply for conscientious-objector status.

Cooch tried to persuade Tom to change his mind, but, unable to sway him, offered, "Let me see if there's anything I can do."

While Cooch explored the options, Tom filed for relief as a conscientious objector. In quintessential Waddell fashion, he answered the army's standard questions with essays that might have befuddled most officers. One question, for instance, asked, "Do you believe in a supreme being?" It was a simple question, but to Tom it was a call to rhetoric.

I do not employ the term "supreme being" in my religious conviction. My religious views are not metaphysical, but ethical, and have been arrived at independent of orthodox religious knowledge. I believe the principles upon which I base all my actions are more substantial than orthodox religious teachings because mine are based on empirical knowledge which can be examined and evaluated in view of personal experience. As Kant has pointed out in his refutation of the cosmological argument: The principle of causality, that every event must have a cause, applies, as far as we can tell, only to the world of sense experience. But in the cosmological argument, this principle about empirical knowledge is used to carry us beyond the world of sense experience to something that is supposed to transcend it. This principle, Kant insisted, is unjustified and illegitimate. We have no basis for assuming that the principles we employ in the analysis of our experience can be made to apply to anything beyond experience.

It is essential in my beliefs to point out that standards of value are derived from experience, for which the only prerequisite is a rational mind. Man has acquired, through evolutionary process, such a capacity (rational thought) and his actions are a direct result of the sum total of his experience, guided by the application of rational thought. Orthodox religious belief fosters the concept that standards of value are the arbitrary pronouncement of God, but I contend that man has created universal standards of value which the conventional Deity accepts and obeys. Plato touched upon this when he asked: Is something right because the gods will it, or do they will it because it is right?

For lack of a better term, I am essentially a humanist, with modifications. Humanism is an attitude which centers on distinctive human interests or ideals, but I carry this one step further. I believe that, in addition to those distinctive traits, which for the most part are culturally derived, there are also instinctive traits. Unfortunately, the distinctive traits can be influenced and changed, particularly so in a mass society (this is well described by William Hauser), but fortunately the instinctive traits are unalterable, though, clearly, they can be suppressed.

The metaphysicist, given his earlier restrictive environment, was forced to give this inward, ethical and moralistic force an external, supernatural meaning and expectedly, an anthropomorphic image which is inescapably a reflection of the fact that this "force" is internally human in nature—man created God in his image!

What is called God or a "Supreme Being," to me, is not something to depend upon for guidance, nor is it something outside of myself that I am in relation to. It is a natural force within me which gives meaning and purpose to my individual self and it is that part of my being which calls for "right-ness" in all actions.

Given my belief in the internally human origin of standards of value and their application through experience, I am faced with decisions, decisions of morality or right-ness. The inherent "ethical being" is challenged and forced to a conclusion, based not on historical or political facts, but on the nature of man himself. Too often, with too many, these decisions are obscured by data irrelevant to man's nature and the decision becomes an "inhuman" one. I regard war as inhuman.

Tom's battles with the military were mostly intellectual, at least on his part, wars of words. But on occasion they turned physical, almost slapstick. Upon receiving his CO application, the army sent Tom to a chaplain at Walter Reed Hospital for review, a standard procedure.

The chaplain, according to Tom, was "just the perfect picture of a colonel and a clergyman." His uniform was spotlessly scrubbed and crisply pressed, and with his white hair and broad smile, he looked positively angelic.

"What is the problem?" the chaplain inquired.

"Well," Tom replied, "I'm an atheist."

The chaplain's back stiffened.

"And I object to the war."

The chaplain wound himself a little tighter. "What do you mean, you object to the war?" he asked.

"Well, I think we're wrong."

"That's not for you to decide," the chaplain counseled, as solicitously as he could.

"Why not?" Tom asked.

"Because you're in the army now," the chaplain said, "and the army tells you what to do."

"Well, maybe I signed a paper saying that, but it's not anything I ever believed in."

The chaplain asked about Tom's background.

Tom explained that he was a radical and that he didn't believe in what the United States had done in Vietnam or, for that matter, in Korea. He said he also disagreed with what the government was doing in Latin America.

He was waving a red flag in front of a patriot.

The chaplain, unable to contain himself any longer, exploded. "You are a dastardly son-of-a-bitch communist!" he screamed. "A pinko communist fag!"

As Tom saw it, the chaplain then sprouted fangs, lunged across his desk, and, bent on strangling this "pinko," chased him around the office shouting, "You son of a bitch!" Tom retreated to the outer office, dashed past the secretaries and soldiers who were watching and listening in shock, and ran out the door. He could hear the chaplain cursing his footsteps.

"I got all kinds of reprimands from the army," Tom recalled, "and of course my application for conscientious objector status was rejected. I was prepared to go to prison."

Even Enge had difficulty following all of Tom's reasoning. "Enge and I have had a major disagreement about what he calls fundamental values," Tom wrote to Steve Schwartz. "In filling out my CO form, I became convinced of a good deal of the pacifist argument. This entered into a discussion I had last weekend with Enge, and he became upset, very upset. He feels that my background is insufficient to make such commitments to a point of view."

Still, Enge tried to be helpful. When the application for CO status was rejected, Enge took Tom to meet his old friend, the columnist Drew Pearson. Enge asked Pearson if he would ring up his contacts in the Department of Defense and put in a word for Tom.

Tom never knew what, if anything, Pearson did, or whether it had any impact, but he did begin receiving daily calls from army intelligence. Under interrogation, he held to his principles, insisting he was morally opposed to the war. He said the army shouldn't expect him to act counter to his moral beliefs.

Suddenly, only a few days before he was scheduled to depart for Vietnam, Tom received new orders: He was to remain at Walter Reed, as assistant director of the global-medicine course.

He later learned that it was Colonel Cooch who had initiated the change in orders. A lieutenant colonel told Tom that he had cut the new orders at Cooch's request, but reluctantly. The lieutenant colonel called Tom a troublemaker, accused him of being misguided, cowardly, and unpatriotic, and warned him that he could still ship him to Vietnam if he chose to. He said the only reason he felt justified in changing Tom's orders was that the army could ill afford another battle in the courtroom.

Tom's timing was fortunate. The army's relationship with the medical profession had already been strained by the Levy case. Not long before Tom began resisting assignment to Vietnam, a dermatologist named Howard Levy, on active military duty, had refused to give Green Beret medics "elementary instruction in skin disease."

Levy, who considered U.S. foreign policy to be "diabolical evil," argued that the Green Berets would use medicine as "another tool of political persuasion," which would be "a complete prostitution of what medicine stands for." He claimed that the army had no control over his mind and will, and could not force him to act counter to his beliefs.

The army chose to take legal action against Levy. He was

court-martialed, charged with disobeying orders and making disloyal statements. The resulting publicity placed the army in an unfavorable light. "The court-martial destroyed some part of the military-medical relationship," Tom said. "A lot of heads rolled as a result."

Tom exploited the Levy case. "I am protesting," he mentioned in his CO application, "because it may point out how the medical profession is being prostituted in this war. We're being asked to serve in a situation where this country is engaged in crimes against humanity."

Though Enge suggested that Pearson had gotten his orders changed, Tom thought that Howard Levy deserved much more of the credit.

Spared from fighting in the war, Tom continued to fight against it. Even while he served as a commissioned officer in the army, he worked for the Central Committee for Conscientious Objectors, advising and counseling applicants from his Washington apartment. He also contributed time and energy to the War Resisters League and the Medical Committee for Human Rights.

He attacked the army from within, too. One of his duties was to teach young doctors about China, and when he saw a film called *China*, a favorable view of the dawn of a new society, produced by a documentary filmmaker named Felix Green, Tom thought it was a perfect educational tool. The army felt it was communist propaganda.

Through the New York offices of the film's distributor, Tom arranged to have Green show *China* to his global-medicine students. When he decided the film was too important to be limited to a small group, he moved the screening from his classroom to the Walter Reed theater and distributed flyers announcing the showing.

On the night of the screening, with the film loaded into

the projector and about to roll, intelligence officers burst into the theater and confiscated the print. They questioned Tom for a week, demanding to know why he wanted to show a "communist" film.

He argued the film's merits, then showed it to a select group of doctors and intelligence officers. "We discussed it afterward," he said, "and the doctors all thought it was a nice film. But the army intelligence people were appalled. 'Waddell, you'd better get in line or you're going to be in a lot of trouble,' they warned me.

"And I'd say, 'Like what?'

"I loved pulling those guys' chains."

During the 1960s, with his studies and his internship, his army days and his causes, Tom's personal life became often little more than an afterthought. Enge remained the central love of his life, but generally, after the mid-sixties, only from afar. He wavered between homosexual encounters and love affairs with women.

During the early sixties Jackie Leonard, one of Tom's friends and benefactors from The Farm, introduced him to her cousin's daughter, a tall, slim, striking redhead with the lyrical name Quenby Sameth. The three of them went ice skating, and Quenby and Tom became first friends, and then more. By the mid-sixties, during Tom's internship, they were sharing an apartment and a bed in New York's teeming drug district, the East Village.

For the second time, Tom became engaged. Quenby knew that Tom loved Enge spiritually, and perhaps physically, but she longed to become his wife. Tom vacillated. He resisted Quenby's love whenever he felt it was too strong and cultivated it whenever she began to pull away. Quenby recognized his uncertainty and his doubts.

"Tom, you have no commitment to me, and I have none

to you," she wrote him one night. "KNOW THIS. When you say to me, 'You are the only one for me,' I hear it as, 'I *think*, right now, that you are the only one for me—but I am *not committing* myself—to *anything*. . . .' This is not to say that I do not take what you say very seriously. It's a beautiful thing to love and be loved, and I know that there are loves which do not last, but which are none the less beautiful for that fact— old Sameth proverb: You can't marry *everyone* you love! So I do not feel that you owe me anything, except a decent amount of honesty.

"In other words, my dear, I am *horrified* . . . at the thought that you might someday feel it incumbent upon you to *marry* me, because (maybe unconsciously) you 'felt obligated,' and you 'had to,' and you 'owed me so much. . . .' "

Eventually Tom broke off the relationship. But shortly after they split up, he proposed to Quenby. She told him she had already accepted another man's proposal, and even though she cried when Tom protested that he had always intended to marry her, she knew better than to depend on him. She married, and Tom said he felt "shitty and depressed."

He then began dating a woman who reminded him of Quenby, and he slept with her, too, but soon abandoned the affair. His relationship with Quenby, like the earlier one with Bea Brown, did not end cheerfully. He did not hear from her for ten years, not until 1976, when he came out of the closet publicly.

While he was at Walter Reed, Tom had a homosexual affair with a researcher he met at a medical conference, a relationship that almost ended before it began, when the researcher spotted a police badge in Tom's wallet. Frightened and confused by the badge, he asked Tom if he was in the CIA. Tom explained that he carried a New York City police surgeon's badge in order to get in and out of the Riker's Island prison.

．　　　．　　　．

Over the 1967 Thanksgiving holiday, Tom played in a touch football game with two of Enge's nephews, Danny Menaker and his brother Mike. During the game Mike Menaker, who had become a good friend of Tom's, aggravated an old knee injury. In December he went to the hospital for simple surgery to remove a piece of torn cartilage. The procedure was routine, but complications quickly developed. A toxic infection ravaged Menaker's body, and he suffered two episodes of cardiac arrest.

Danny Menaker later wrote of Mike's struggle in a short story called "Brothers." In the story, Danny's name was Dave, and Mike's was Nicholas:

> Nicholas turned his face back toward Dave. He said, firmly, "Davey, this is it." He took a deep breath, like someone who is about to swim down to the bottom of a lake to find something valuable he has lost there, and then he died.

Mike Menaker's death was almost as painful for Tom as it was for Danny.

In January 1968, in his final year in the army, Tom put a small down payment on a $43,000 house on Thirty-fifth Street N.W. in Washington, anticipating a year of senior residency at Georgetown University after his discharge. Steve Schwartz, who had returned safely from Vietnam, shared the house with him. Schwartz did not suspect that Tom, who was dating several women at the time, was gay, but some of his friends did, and their suspicions annoyed Steve.

October 13, 1984

It has been a year since I last wrote in your book. Too much
has happened, and all our lives have been complicated. I
sometimes fear that I complicate others' rather than they
complicate mine.

I have been doing quite a bit of traveling in the past year.
One trip was to Vancouver to speak at their second Gay Summer Games. It was only three days, but I saw old friends and
was warmly greeted by the community—one of those pleasurable perks one gets when committed to an action that informs
or elevates.

I feel like a teacher, and my reward is not material, but
the pleasure I get in allowing people to feel their self-esteem.
Strangely enough, it is a principle that I seem to apply best
to a crowd. I sometimes doubt that I do it for my friends. I
must think about that. Thank you for pointing it out to me,
Jessica.

Another trip was to Winnipeg, Manitoba (you'll probably
get to know these Canadian cities—you may in the future be
a Canadian since Mom is Canadian), where the small gay
community, or rather some of its enthusiasts, invited me to
speak about exercise and health, again because of the notoriety from the Games. There was a reception honoring me as
the founder of the Games. It all sounded like satisfying fun
and so I went.

Only about five people attended the reception, and my
hosts, who were very British about it, were interminably
apologetic. I was not offended. I was pleased to have some
quiet time to myself. I went to the Museum of Nature and
was delighted for a very short hour. I taped two TV shows
with a gay activist who was host of his own show. Good questions and fun to answer.

I show your pictures and talk about you wherever I go.
The third trip was September 15–30. It was not without

problems. I was asked to go to Africa by a man named John Hall, one of the Dunies [the Dunesmen, a group of politically active and influential gays in San Francisco, including Tom, Zohn and Jim Hormel, who periodically gathered for a retreat at Pajaro Dunes on the central California coast]. We had dated and found each other interesting—at least I was aware that he was teaching me something, but I'm not sure he was learning anything from me. But I will ask him.

I hesitated because of Zohn and you and Mom—and the Games. Then I figured you and Mom could handle it— particularly since Mom knew I had been under a lot of stress lately. Her response was: AFRICA? I could see her thinking of the Dark Continent, full of danger and lurking death, and snakes! She couldn't understand why anyone would want to go to AFRICA! But she was easy to convince. I told her how beautiful and exciting it is—and how safe it is.

The Games—they would just have to wait.

But Zohn. I knew he would feel hurt and that was my big hesitation. But things have been bad around here. When I'm not with you, and that is about half the week, I work on the Games, for the American Civil Liberties Union, write articles for *Coming Up*, work on the house, meet people who want to use the hall for an event.

I run around all over the place working for non-profit organizations and projects. All non-remunerative. At times, I think I'm crazy for what I'm doing and ask myself what am I doing this for. And I don't really know.

On the other hand, I believe the Games are important.

The track-and-field team that represented the United States in the 1968 Olympic Games in Mexico City may have been the strongest in history.

Lee Evans sprinted 400 meters so swiftly that his time—43.86 seconds—remained the world record for almost twenty years.

Bob Beamon long-jumped so far that his distance—29 feet 2 1/2 inches—shattered the world record by almost two feet. His record endured for more than twenty years.

Al Oerter, for the fourth Olympics in a row, threw the discus farther than he had ever thrown it before, and for the fourth Olympics in a row earned the gold medal.

Dick Fosbury, with his Fosbury Flop, set an Olympic record in the high jump.

Sprinters James Hines and Tommie Smith each set a world record—Hines at 100 meters, Smith at 200.

Hurdler Willie Davenport broke the Olympic record in his event and later became only the second American to compete in both the summer and the winter Games.

They were Tom Waddell's Olympic teammates in Mexico City. "I was awed by anything Olympic," he once said. "Totally, totally awed. To be on an Olympic team with people who were heroes to me, people I stood in awe of—suddenly, I'm their teammate. I was thirty years old, and I had to keep pinching myself and asking myself, *Is this real?*"

Less than a year before the 1968 Games began, Tom Waddell was an army physician who seemed to be a more logical candidate for a court-martial than for the U.S. Olympic team.

"He refused to go to Vietnam and he took part in antiwar demonstrations," said his college teammate Jack Savoia. "He was an embarrassment to the army, so they sent him to train just to get rid of him."

At thirty Tom had not competed in a decathlon in almost six years, or in any athletic event in more than four years. He was teaching global medicine at Walter Reed Hospital when, spurred by the urge to get back in shape, and by the urge to compete, he decided on his comeback.

He began training early in 1968, running five miles each morning, lifting weights, and playing touch football with his students. He knew that the scoring system in the decathlon had been changed since he tried out for the 1960 Olympic team, and that the new scoring tables rewarded his strengths, especially the javelin and the high jump.

He applied for a transfer to the army's track-and-field team, and in May 1968 he was ordered to Fort MacArthur, in San Pedro, California, to begin training full-time for the 1968 U.S. Olympic team. "We worked out every day, all day," Tom said. "We had no other duties, and all the weight-training equipment in the world."

Tom lived in the team barracks—its oldest athlete, and the highest-ranking officer. Some of his fellow soldiers were far more accomplished athletes. Mel Pender, for one, was among the world's fastest sprinters. Tom had a long way to go to catch up; he worked out as many as twelve hours a day.

In his first meet as a thirty-year-old, on June 6, at UCLA, Tom accumulated 6,969 points, a personal best, good enough for him to finish second in the meet, but still a long way from Olympic standards.

During the competition he met a representative of one of the major footwear companies and asked for a pair of free track shoes. Shoes were commonly offered to athletes, often with a few dollars stuffed inside as a bonus for wearing the brand. The shoe rep asked Tom what his best score was in the decathlon, and when Tom told him, he laughed and recommended that Tom wear a competitor's brand. The insult rankled, and he promised himself he wouldn't forget.

In his second decathlon competition, Tom's Olympic hopes took a bad beating. He had a strong first day, including a pair of personal records (PRs), which lifted him into second place behind Bill Toomey. But on the second day he ruined his score with a disastrous performance in the pole vault.

He cleared twelve feet six inches during his warm-up, and in the competition he decided to skip the lower heights and start at eleven feet. Like Dan O'Brien in the U.S. Olympic trials a quarter of a century later, Tom failed three times to clear his opening height. Shut out in the pole vault, he managed only 6,448 points, well below the 7,200 needed to qualify for the Olympic trials.

The army had to petition the United States Olympic Committee even to consider Tom for the trials. The USOC agreed, but set certain conditions. First he had to enter three pole-vault competitions prior to the trials and clear at least thirteen feet each time. He did. Then he needed to score a minimum of 7,200 points, well above his personal best, in a decathlon at Mount San Antonio College, a track-and-field shrine between Los Angeles and San Diego. If he came up short, his Olympic hopes would be dashed, and the army could order him back to Washington or even to Vietnam.

Tom responded to the pressure brilliantly. He felt "like Superman," he said, perhaps the result of moving from the high altitude of San Pedro to the low altitude of southern California. He amassed 7,587 points, the second-best decathlon score in the United States that year and the fifth best in the world.

"He burst from obscurity," reported *Track & Field News*, the sport's journal of record.

Even the shoe company representative was impressed. He approached Tom after the 1,500-meter run, the final event of the decathlon, and offered him two dozen pairs of shoes. Free.

"Do you think they'll fit up your ass?" Tom inquired.

Tom's performance at Mount San Antonio earned him an invitation to the Olympic trials at South Lake Tahoe. He was one of ten decathletes competing for the three berths on the U.S. team. The ten trained together in Tahoe, at 7,400 feet above sea level, matching the conditions in Mexico City. They encouraged and coached one another, nurturing a cooperative spirit rare among athletes contending for such a coveted prize, but not rare among decathletes.

"Decathletes would always get together and have lots of

fun together," Tom said. "They would help each other out because they weren't really competing against each other. They
were competing against themselves."

This was precisely what drew Tom to the decathlon, the
challenge of proving himself to himself, plus, of course, the
chance to be the athletic version of a Renaissance man, practicing such conflicting disciplines as sprinting and shot
putting—one rewarding mass, the other punishing it.

The ten events within the decathlon are, in order, the
100-meter dash, the long jump, the shot put, the high jump
and the 400-meter dash on the first day, and the 110-meter
hurdles, the discus, the pole vault, the javelin, and the grueling
1,500-meter run on the second day. The decathlon is, as
Brooks Johnson suggested, the most "macho" of track-and-
field events, demanding speed, strength, and stamina in almost
equal doses.

Almost no one ever records personal bests in all ten
events during a two-day decathlon competition; even three or
four PRs is extraordinary, a rare and immensely satisfying
experience.

"The decathlon is the most social of track events," Frank
Zarnowski wrote in *The Decathlon*, his definitive history of the
event, "and promotes a strong sense of camaraderie among
contestants. There is a lot of time to visit during and between
events, much of which is used in helping other participants.
Athletes will give and take advice, analyze each other's technique, assist each other in locating and checking take-off
points, and even use each other's equipment."

In 1960, for example, the two best decathletes in the
world, Rafer Johnson of the United States and C. K. Yang of
Taiwan, were each other's fiercest rivals—and best friends.
During the 1980s Jürgen Hingsen of West Germany and
Daley Thompson of Great Britain carried on a rivalry marked
by great wit and by Thompson's head-to-head dominance. By
the 1990s, both men were broadcasters, delighting in each

other's company. "Daley, you have gray hair now," Hingsen needled over dinner one night, and Thompson, twice the Olympic champion, countered, "Jürgen, so do you. But the difference is, I gave you yours."

Tom Waddell was not only a competitor at South Lake Tahoe in 1968; he was also the team physician, which earned him a private cabin and access to both steroids and the means to inject them. He was often asked by world-class athletes to give them injections they were afraid to give themselves.

In 1968 the track-and-field world had not yet outlawed steroids, and they were widely used, at least experimentally. "I would say half the team was on steroids," Tom recalled. "Very, very popular." He recognized the potentially damaging long-term side effects and limited himself to small doses of an oral steroid, five milligrams a day compared with the twenty to twenty-five milligrams some athletes injected. Still, he was impressed by the drug; he beefed up noticeably and claimed he felt the effects immediately.

"There was widespread use of analgesics, anti-inflammatory drugs, anabolic steroids, cortisone . . . and the most gross abuse of vitamins and minerals that I have ever encountered," Tom wrote in the *Maryland State Medical Journal* after the Olympics. "I . . . saw athletes eating up to 10,000 mg of vitamin C in a single day."

Many of Tom's teammates went to him for medical counsel and information. "Tom answered the questions evenly," recalled Phil Shinnick, a long jumper in Tahoe who later became a researcher in sports medicine, "and everyone felt he could bare his soul to him. Tom himself had a great soul, and we could see it in his eyes."

Shinnick had enormous respect for Tom. "Of the thousands of athletes I've met," he wrote in the New York *Times*, "no one developed his potential as much as Tom Waddell, an Olympian, musician, artist, physician and healer."

Tom took his own risks in Tahoe. Every time he pole-vaulted, he jeopardized his shoulders. His technique was atrocious, his determination substantial, and that combination—no style and considerable substance—put tremendous strain on the shoulders. He suffered frequent separations and chronic pain.

"I knew at the time I was damaging myself," he said, "but I made a decision. I said, 'Look, you are going to have arthritis and you are going to have pain—what do you want to do? Do you want to stop now and not have pain, or can you live with it?' I said, 'Screw it, I'm going to live with it. I'm not stopping now.'"

The Olympic trials took place at the end of the first week of September, six weeks before the Games in Mexico City. Tom did not go into the competition ranked among the top three candidates. Four or five of his rivals possessed better credentials than he, and all of them were younger. Still, Tom was confident. He knew that he thrived on pressure, that he performed better in competition than in practice. His adrenaline helped him in front of crowds; he was more than an athlete, he was a showman.

But on the first day he exceeded even his own expectations. He started off with a lackluster 100 meters, then finished second in the long jump, the high jump and the shot put, and completed the day with a personal best of 49.8 seconds in the 400-meter run, the fourth-fastest time of the day. After five events, Tom was second to Bill Toomey in the overall standings.

He started strongly the next day, running the hurdles in 14.8 seconds—another personal record—followed by impressive performances in the discus and javelin, and a respectable showing of thirteen feet five and one-half inches in the pole vault.

Tom came to the final event, the 1,500-meter run, knowing that only collapse could keep him from scoring enough points to make the United States Olympic team. And when he finished the race, he had 7,706 points, a personal best by far, and the third berth on the U.S. team, behind Toomey, who had barely missed the world record, and Rick Sloan.

Tom had outscored Toomey in three events—the high jump, the shot put, and the pole vault.

"He should not have made the team," Toomey said almost twenty years later, "but he did. Because he's that kind of guy. He's indefatigable. When he sets his mind on something, it happens.

"I'll never forget him in Tahoe. He was tough. He was great. He came through like a bandito."

Surrounded by superstars, by world-record holders, Tom suspected he was out of his league on the Olympic team. "I was a decent high-school athlete," he said. "I was a decent college athlete. But that's all. At Springfield you could be a star with no talent, and that's basically what I was."

For once, Tom underestimated himself. He may not have been a great athlete, but he was a very good one, and his work ethic turned him into an overachiever. He was also a remarkably graceful athlete. "Tom was the second most beautifully coordinated man I ever saw," said Jack Sussman, his friend from The Farm. "The first was Joe DiMaggio."

When Tom marched in the opening ceremonies in the Olympic Stadium, wearing his U.S.A. uniform, he smiled broadly and waved to the crowd. "It felt like I was walking on a cloud," he said. "I was an Olympian. Have you ever listened to a rock-and-roll star and fantasized, *That's me up there. I'm strumming my guitar and everyone's going crazy?* That's what the Olympics were for me."

Still, as excited as Tom was about being a part of the

Olympic Games, he was not blind to the event's faults. He supported the black American athletes who protested racism in the United States, and he sympathized with the Mexican students who protested the extravagance and wastefulness of the Games.

In the summer of 1968, in the months leading up to the Olympics, the war between the Mexican government and the university students began with small, sporadic battles. The students demonstrated against the country's low rate of literacy and high rate of crime, against the squalor of its slums and the severity of its police; and against an economic system that seemed rigged to make the rich steadily richer and the poor angrily poorer.

Only two weeks before the Games were to begin, the government made what appeared to be a conciliatory move: The troops that had been occupying Mexico City's two main university campuses were withdrawn. On October 2, ten days before the opening ceremonies, students organized a rally in a public square called the Plaza of the Three Cultures.

At first the rally was impassioned but peaceful. Then, in the early evening, army helicopters dropped green flares on the plaza, and within minutes, a thousand soldiers and riot police had charged into the square. The crowd, perhaps 5,000, panicked, and in the chaos soldiers and police clubbed and clawed the students. The battle went on for almost an hour, and when the shooting and the fighting finally stopped, more than 30 students were dead, more than 100 others injured, and more than 300 headed for jail.

Many of the international athletes who came to Mexico City did not know about the students who died. But Tom did, and he sought out Anita Weissburg, a friend of Enge's who lived in Mexico City. She took him to the Plaza of the Three Cultures, showed him the bullet holes and the blood that still stained the street. Tom talked to survivors, listened to them complain bitterly that a Third World country like Mexico, with so many of its citizens suffering economically, had no business hosting an opulent athletic spectacle.

Tom understood their feelings, and the feelings of the black American Olympians who had at one time considered boycotting the Games to protest racism in the United States. In Mexico City Tom wrote press releases for the black athletes, encouraged them, cheered for them. He would have done more if Harry Edwards, the sociologist and activist who had triggered the black athletes' revolt, had not barred whites from the final meetings that determined what actions the athletes would take in Mexico City. Tom's civil-rights credentials carried little weight with Edwards, who seemed to thrive on antiwhite rhetoric.

On October 16, eight men lined up for the final of the 200-meter dash. Three of them were Americans, and two, Tommie Smith and John Carlos, were blacks from San Jose State, where Edwards taught sociology and anthropology.

Carlos bolted into the early lead, but then Smith sped past him and won the race. An Australian placed second, Carlos third. When the medalists stood upon the victory stand, Smith and Carlos both had their sweatpants legs rolled up, exposing long black socks and no shoes. And as "The Star-Spangled Banner" was played, Smith, on the top rung of the stand, pulled his right hand out of his windbreaker and raised it high; Carlos, on the bottom rung, pulled out his left hand and raised it as well. Each clenched his fist in protest, and each fist wore a black glove. Both men's heads were bowed, ignoring the national anthem and the American flag. They said their unshod feet represented black poverty, and their raised fists demonstrated black strength and black unity.

Their boldness and their bitterness enraged the United States Olympic Committee. The USOC formally apologized for the two athletes' actions, claiming the country was embarrassed by their "untypical exhibitionism" and "immature behavior" that "violates the basic standards of sportsmanship and good manners which are so highly regarded in the United States." In a vivid demonstration of the USOC's insensitivity to racial tensions, Smith and Carlos were swiftly shipped back to the States, their athletic careers smeared, their lives and characters stained.

Tom Waddell quickly voiced his defense of Smith and Carlos. "I was pleased by their protest," he announced. "I was afraid they weren't going to do it. I was disappointed more Negro athletes backed down."

His comments appeared in the international press. When he was asked if the athletes' actions had discredited the American flag, Tom countered, "I think they have been discredited by the flag more often than they have discredited it." And when he was asked if the United States' image had been tarnished, he replied, "Our image is so bad it can't get any worse. Maybe this will help."

Hazel Waddell, Tom's adoptive mother, was asked by a New Jersey newspaper to comment on his remarks. "That sounds normal for him," she said.

The army, of course, was not amused. Three days after the Smith and Carlos protest, just as Tom was about to begin the second day of decathlon competition, a stranger walked up to him, grabbed his arm and informed him that Colonel Don Miller, the military liaison to all army personnel on the Olympic team, had ordered him court-martialed for the comments that had appeared in the New York *Times* and the Washington *Post*.

"Talk to me tomorrow," Tom said, and went off to run the 110-meter hurdles.

No one ever followed up on the threat of a court-martial.

If Tom had run a little more swiftly, he would have won the gold medal in the 1968 Olympic decathlon. In five field events—the shot put, high jump, discus, pole vault, and javelin—he turned in better performances than Bill Toomey.

But in the four running events and the long jump, an event that also puts a premium on speed, Toomey's performances were far better than Tom's. Tom had the slowest 100 meters, the slowest 400, and the third-slowest hurdles and 1,500 meters among the top-eight Olympic decathletes.

Still, he had much to be proud of. On the first day he posted personal records in the long jump, shot put, and high jump. On the second day he had personal bests in the discus and the pole vault. His total score—7,719 points—beat his previous best by thirteen points; it was, at the time, one of the top-ten scores ever recorded by an American. He finished second among Americans in Mexico City—Rick Sloan trailed him by twenty-seven points—and he was sixth among thirty-three competitors from twenty countries.

For Tom, it was a magnificent showing. "I couldn't have been happier if I had won," he said.

For Bill Toomey, it was even better. Toomey took the lead right at the start of the decathlon, with a sizzling 100-meter sprint and a terrific long jump. At the end of the first day he had amassed more points than anyone in the history of the event. On the second day he did fine in the hurdles and the discus. Then came the pole vault. The bar was set at the opening height of eleven feet nine and a quarter inches, normally a cinch for Toomey. But he missed on his first try, and again on his second. If he failed once more, he could forget about any medal, much less a gold.

"I had done so many things wrong on my first two jumps," Toomey said years later, "I couldn't figure out how to correct anything. Everything was closing in on me—the people in that huge arena, the people watching on television back home, my whole life, all the years of working and waiting for this moment. If I missed, it would be like dying."

Toomey soared over the bar on his third attempt, and went

on to clear thirteen feet nine and a half inches, his best vault ever in competition. He set an Olympic record for the decathlon and won the gold, and Tom Waddell could not have been more delighted.

"There really was no room for jealousy," Tom said. "When I saw Bill on the victory stand, I felt as if I were sharing the medal."

Of course, Tom thought he might have done better; decathletes always do. "The decathlete never nears perfection, is seldom completely satisfied, almost always finishes a bit frustrated," wrote Frank Zarnowski. "No matter how well he does, no matter the win or the record, he can always find room for improvement in several of the events. There is always a 'Wait until next time' attitude."

But Tom had come as close to his own perfection as he ever had. He was eager to "wait until next time," to start thinking about the 1972 Olympics in Munich. In 1969 he was profiled in the first issue of *Rx Sports and Travel*, a leisure magazine aimed at physicians. The story, "**DR. TOM WADDELL: OLYMPIAN**," ends with the young physician contemplating his future. He mentions a residency at Georgetown University and the possibility of working for the World Health Organization or the United Nations. He says he might like to teach medicine in a developing nation. He admits that his chances of making the Olympic team in 1972 are not strong. "After all," says Dr. Tom Waddell, "I am thirty-one years old, and I still have to find a wife."

He had found a friend in Mexico City, a young woman named Marjorie Margolies, a television reporter who covered the Games for the CBS affiliate in Philadelphia. She was looking for a good story when she chanced upon Tom, and she was smart enough to know she had found one. She hung out with Tom and Toomey in Mexico, and when she returned to Philadelphia, and Tom to Washington, they saw each other occasionally.

December 8, 1984

Tonight, my darling, there was a raffle for the Games. I had done most of the arranging and detailing. It was an important victory for me, restoring my self-confidence which has been on the wane lately. Zohn was very helpful, as usual. He always pitches in, it is in his nature, and while it is something that everyone loves about Zohn, it's something we all use.

Zohn is a wonderful man. He's magical because he's a child, and he makes us all want to be children. But there is one thing about being a child that is given up in adulthood—and that is dependency. I realize, sweetheart, that I am projecting my feelings into some kind of truth—and I find at the same time that "truth" is a very elusive concept. We use it to serve our needs—and sometimes it does not serve us well.

Zohn and I have been having a lot of difficulty in our relationship, and we are both miserable. I have a lot on my shoulders now. I am being sued by the USOC, the United States Olympic Committee, for $96,000 [for using the term Gay "Olympics"], and while I think it is unlikely that I'll have to pay it, there is a terrible anxiety about it.

Enge is now eighty-nine years old, very feeble, and very lonely. I call him every week, but it is always a difficult conversation. I try to fight my guilt feelings about not being in N.Y. with him.

My dad, your grandfather Elmer, has cancer, and it has spread to his spine and hip and he is in great pain. I call him about every day and am trying to convince him to come to S.F. He is alone, except for my younger brother Rick.

I am looking for a part-time job to ease my financial burdens. Mom and I took you to the Montessori School for an

interview—you can't start till age 2 1/2, but you need to reg-
ister soon. Nancy Achilles [a friend of Tom's] will pay for
your schooling just because she wants to. Still, I need to start
making money again so I can do more to the house and afford
some of the extra things I want for myself and your future—
like a computer.

I want to finish the Games in 1986—and I cannot get
paid for that work—I don't mind not getting paid, but I dislike doing most of the work and raising most of the money—
yuck—let me get off this. In any case, the pressures these
days leave me wanting to be alone whenever there's an opportunity. I want to write and read, but there is so little time,
and Zohn would like the time I do have. I am really torn
about the appropriateness of my behavior toward Zohn. He
feels abandoned and there is some truth to that. He likes to
take over, and I am not one to be taken over—so I have
stepped back and it has not been pleasant.

Suellen Manning was not impressed. Not by Dr. Tom
Waddell's credentials, not by his appearance. Athlete, soldier,
world traveler, physician. "Great, just what we need," she said.
"Another good-looking, cocky ex-jock doctor."

Suellen was the head nurse on 2-South at Georgetown
University Hospital, and she had too many patients, too much
responsibility, to nursemaid another neophyte who was, in all
likelihood, full of himself. She was prepared to dislike Tom
heartily, until, during his early days at the hospital, he walked
headfirst into a pair of automatic doors, slicing a bloody gash
in his forehead. Suellen stitched him up and decided he might
not be so bad after all. At least he wasn't perfect.

She liked him even better after he invited her to his house
for dinner and taught her to play Fictionary, an intellectual
parlor game he had learned at The Farm which demands defi-
nitions of obscure words.

The nurse and the doctor became friends, and the friendship grew into something more. They enjoyed what Tom called "a low-maintenance relationship," which meant that their feelings remained the same whether they were in the same room or a thousand miles apart, or whether they saw each other daily or yearly. Tom thought this was the best kind of love.

Suellen Manning had also been raised as a Catholic. She shared Tom's doubts about religion, and his hunger for adventure, and delighted in his company. He opened her up to new ideas and new information, much as Enge had done for him almost a decade earlier. Tom took her to The Farm, introduced her to Enge, and she fell under the man's spell, finding him simultaneously intimidating and fascinating—so much so that a few years later, after Tom had migrated west, she moved from Washington to The Farm and lived there for nine months, recuperating from another love affair.

Tom put in a year as a junior resident at Georgetown, a year spiced, typically, by a track-and-field trip to Germany and the Soviet Union—he was both U.S. team doctor and team member, and Brooks Johnson and Phil Shinnick were again among his teammates—and by a variety of interests. He volunteered his services to the Medical Committee for Human Rights in Washington, which was trying to upgrade treatment in the black ghettos of the District of Columbia, and he also devoted time to the United States Olympic Committee.

Despite his Mexico City activism and his support of Smith and Carlos, the USOC enlisted Tom as a medical consultant, a position that prompted him to offer the committee advice on almost every subject. Tom suggested that the men's and women's teams be combined, that curfews be abolished, that athletes choose their own trainers and coaches, and that the USOC place greater emphasis on human rights. He also argued that Olympic athletes should be paid during training, that outdated concepts of amateurism should be discarded. "The Olympics is full-time," he said, "like a business." Many of his ideas have since been put into practice.

He also interrupted his Georgetown tour for an abbreviated excursion to South Carolina. He teamed up with another physician who opposed the war in Vietnam, and they went to a small off-coast island, inhabited by blacks who lived primitively, spoke their own language, and were about to be drafted into the U.S. Army. The doctors intended to examine the blacks and pronounce them physically unfit for the draft.

They set up their clinic and, just as they were to begin the examinations, there was a loud and impatient knock at the door. A local redneck and his committee of vigilantes pushed their way into the clinic, carrying ropes. "You and your cronies," their leader informed Tom, "you got a half hour to get out of South Carolina."

Tom and his cronies beat the deadline. The words and the ropes were very persuasive.

After a year at Georgetown, Tom returned to Montefiore Hospital in the Bronx, this time as a senior resident. He concentrated on his assignment when he wasn't helping the Black Panthers set up a health clinic in the Bedford-Stuyvesant section of Brooklyn.

In April 1970, Tom made his second trip to the Soviet Union. He said it was the only international trip he ever paid for with his own money, and he brought with him his mentor and lover, Frederich Engels Menaker.

Incredibly, Enge had never been to Russia. He had always worshipped from a distance. He loved the idea of Russia, loved its culture and its history, loved Chekhov and Tolstoy and Lenin and socialism. He often reminisced about his roots in Odessa and Vilna. But he had never personally experienced any of it.

Tom and Enge traveled throughout the Soviet Union for a month, to Moscow and Leningrad and Odessa; and near the shores of the Black Sea, not far from the Potemkin Steps, they went to the Odessa Opera House and saw a stirring performance of *Eugene Onegin*. It was probably the last extended and pleasurable period that the two men spent together, and it visibly lifted Enge's spirits. For a year, he spoke of little else.

A few weeks after he returned from Russia, Tom traveled for almost a month with Bill Toomey to Central and South America and Africa. The tour was sponsored by the Peace Corps and the Amateur Athletic Union, and its object was to promote physical education. Waddell and Toomey gave seminars on hygiene, nutrition, and preventive medicine, and demonstrations of track-and-field technique.

Toomey not only was the reigning Olympic champion; he had raised the world record in the decathlon to 8,417 points and he was the 1969 winner of the Sullivan Award, presented annually to the nation's outstanding amateur athlete.

Track & Field News commented on the two-man tour:

> If a preconceived jock image existed, it was soon dispelled. The witty Toomey and his articulate sidekick were as quick and sure with their answers (on everything from athletic injuries to the sensitive introspection of what makes a champion) as they were with their hands and feet. Both athletes appeared in enviable if not top condition. Surprisingly, Waddell, sixth at Mexico City, did not play second fiddle to Toomey. He impressed with an overall consistency and virtual mastery of all events. He left no one in doubt as to the championship caliber of this intellectual.

Toomey was as much impressed by Tom as *Track & Field News* was. "It would always stagger me that all of a sudden, if he had to dance, he could start dancing," Toomey said, "and he could draw and he could paint, and I thought, *You know, I'm supposed to be the world's greatest athlete, and here I am traveling with the world's most eclectic person.*"

During his year at Montefiore, Tom saw a great deal of Marjorie Margolies, the television correspondent he had met

Even as a child, Tom wanted
to make people smile . . .

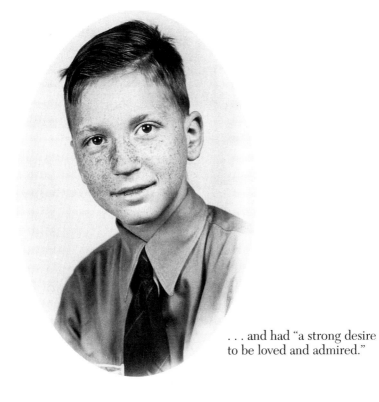

APRIL 16, 1939

TOMMY

. . . and had "a strong desire
to be loved and admired."

Tom's father, Elmer Flubacher (left), was deeply hurt when Tom changed his name to Waddell in gratitude to Gene Waddell of The Three Jacksons (Gene is the one standing on his hands).

To Tommy
best wishes always
The Three Jacksons

THE
3
JACKSONS
Atop the Empire State Buildi

Tom himself performed his own balancing act at a less dizzying height.

At Springfield College, Tom (second from left in both photos) excelled in gymnastics exhibitions and in gymnastics competitions. He loved to be in front of an audience.

Despite the vast difference in their ages and in their backgrounds . . .

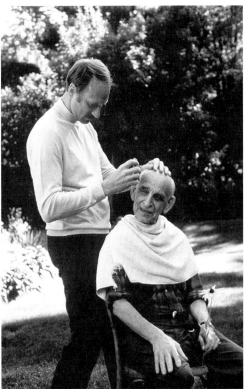

. . . Enge Menaker remained for a quarter of a century the love of Tom's life.

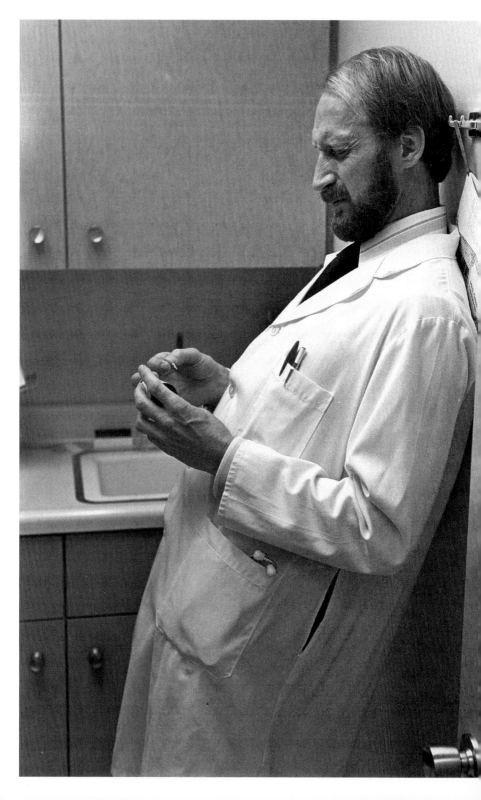

One of medicine's appeals to Tom was that he could carry his job on his back.

Suellen Manning was delighted to discover that Tom wasn't perfect.

The Army decided that instead of training for the war in Vietnam, Tom could train for the Olympic Games in Mexico City.

Tom stood next to his friend Brooks Johnson before one track-and-field tour, and in front of his friend Bill Toomey (wearing sunglasses) in another athletic gathering.

Tom looked as if he could pose for a classical statue of a discus thrower.

The decathlon, with its dueling demands for speed and strength, is the ultimate test of athletic versatility. Tom may not have been "The World's Greatest Athlete," but he was close.

Tom's relationship with Charles Deaton was "a continuing balancing act."

Tom campaigned tirelessly for Gay Games I, editing the
"O-word" out of banners . . .

. . . and posing with
San Francisco's Mayor
Dianne Feinstein and
Zohn Artman.

Tom and Sara took a stroll together for gay rights and pride.

Sara was "an amazingly beautiful and determined woman,"
and Tom embraced her on both counts.

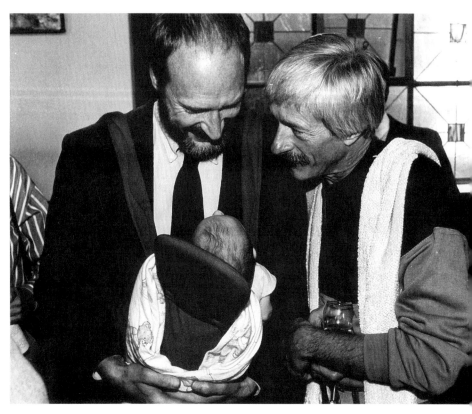

"You're so delicate and charming and bright as a precious stone"—
Tom glowed with pride when he showed off Jessica to Zohn, and she
seemed every bit as pleased with her dad.

in Mexico City. She came to New York at the same time as Tom to attend Columbia University on a CBS fellowship. She never got to visit The Farm, but she was introduced to Enge at the apartment he maintained in New York. Often, when Tom went off on a trip, he returned with a gift for Marjorie; he brought her a jeweled gold necklace from Africa that she wore for years afterward.

Her relationship with Tom, she said, was "a very, very close friendship," but, like several of the women in his life, she knew that something—"an electricity"—was missing. She later married a politician, then became one herself, was elected to the Congress from Pennsylvania and, as the Honorable Marjorie Margolies-Medvinsky, cast the decisive vote for President Clinton's budget in 1993.

Late in 1970, his residency completed, Tom decided to move to California to attend Stanford University on a graduate fellowship. Enge, growing older and crankier, stubbornly opposed the move. He insisted that Tom would lose touch with culture and sensibility in the uncivilized West. He also seemed to fear that Tom would lose touch with him.

Tom acknowledged his need to be independent, and conceded that he was no longer "in love" with Enge exactly as he had been. "It's true that I don't have the insatiable need that I once had," Tom told Enge in a letter from California, "but I do love you quantitatively as well as qualitatively more than anyone else in my life."

Tom invariably expressed his love in his letters from the West Coast.

> I have a short break from my lab work and have the urge to write. As I was walking here from seeing a patient, I suddenly imagined you with a hoe in your hands, working the garden out back. It brought to mind . . . a photo-

graph of you standing in the middle of the garden with a
hoe—you were heavy, about 140 pounds, and you looked
very happy. It was taken some time ago, by me, when
Glen was still alive. After I took the picture, I pretended
to shoot you with my rake; you dropped the hoe and
rolled down the incline to the edge of the road and lay
there till I came running over, laughing, and so in
love. . . .

Less than a year after he left the East, Tom wrote to Enge:
"You need a rest and you need to be away—and I don't mean
New York or Boston. I mean out here! I would like you to
come out and *expect* to do nothing but relax and enjoy yourself. I want to show you the area, I want you to go to the
mountains, the beach, see a movie, spend time at the library,
at the theater in Berkeley, come with me when I work out."

At Stanford, Tom's studies centered upon infectious diseases, including sexually transmitted viruses such as herpes,
and in 1973 he coauthored a paper that was published in the
prestigious *New England Journal of Medicine.* The paper, written with three other physicians, was entitled "Adverse Effect
of Cytosine Arabinoside on Disseminated Zoster in a Con-
trolled Trial." It began, ominously, in those days before there
was any hint of AIDS: "In patients with a compromised immune system, herpes zoster can be a serious and potentially
fatal disease." During the 1980s and 1990s, ironically, people
with AIDS often developed herpes zoster, which is more commonly known as shingles; Tom was one of them.

Between research and study, Tom took flying lessons. "I
got into the air, flew across the mountains to the west and
went a few miles out to sea," he wrote to Enge. "The solitude
was therapeutic, and my concentration on the operation of the
plane allowed me to leave all my problems back on the
ground."

To support himself and his hobbies, he joined a group of

physicians who worked in the emergency rooms of hospitals surrounding the Bay Area. The doctors could set their own schedules, which was fine with Tom, because he needed time to train for the 1972 Olympic Games.

"I want that gold medal so bad I can taste it," he was quoted as saying in *Glamour* magazine in 1972. But neither the sentiment nor the words sounded like Tom's. Certainly, he always wanted to do his best, and always tried to win—Eric Wilkinson recalled that he hated to lose even at Fictionary— but it wasn't medals that motivated him. At least one of the comments attributed to Tom in the same article did ring true, however: "One of the things I want to prove is that you don't have to stop being an athlete just because you're past thirty."

In his final years of competition, he represented the Bay Area Striders, a track club spawned by the Oakland-based In- stitute for the Study of Sport and Society, a haven for athletic radicals founded by Jack Scott, a sports psychologist, sociolo- gist, and therapist who in the mid-1970s harbored the fugitive heiress Patty Hearst. "As part of what we thought should be an athletic revolution," said Phil Shinnick of the Striders, "no one other than active athletes was involved in the operation of the club."

"We had discussion workshops on the relevance of sports in our world," Tom said. "What does it mean to compete in athletic events in a world where there is pollution, racism, and everything else we're aware of?"

He blew out his knee high-jumping in Honolulu early in 1972—"I landed in the pit," he said, "with my kneecap half- way up my thigh"—and did not get to compete in the Olympic trials in Eugene, Oregon. He spoke of trying for the Olympics again in 1976, but he knew his competitive career in track and field was over, suspended, anyway, until the birth of the Gay Games.

While competing, flying, studying, and writing, Tom man- aged to forge and maintain a relationship in the early 1970s, his first with any man other than Enge. Lee Bryan was a few years older than Tom, a southerner, educated in boarding schools, who worked for the Kaiser Foundation, the company that pioneered health maintenance. Tom, too, was employed by Kaiser in the early seventies, primarily treating the company's executives.

Suellen Manning moved to California in 1971, at Tom's urging, and soon after she arrived, he felt secure enough to tell her what he had told no other woman, and few men: that he was gay. Their friendship easily hurdled the revelation and flourished. Suellen lived for a few months in the apartment Tom shared with Lee Bryan. She described Lee as "quiet and meticulous and very obviously gay."

Eventually, the relationship between Tom and Lee turned stormy, regressing on Tom's part from affection to dependency to rejection. They liked each other, then lived with each other, then rejected each other. "I want you to get to know him better," Tom had told Enge early in the relationship. "He reminds me of Glen." But as the relationship deteriorated, Tom said, their conversations grew bitter. "I don't want any part of you," Lee would tell Tom.

"But Lee, I love you, how can you leave me? How can you do this when I love you so?"

"You love me? You call this love? You want to own me."

They broke up, reconciled, and finally separated for good. Tom was so hurt and angry that in later years he refused to talk about Lee or referred to him only as someone he had grossly misjudged, someone he considered evil. "I just wiped him out of my life," Tom said.

Yet when their relationship was approaching its end in 1973, when Tom elected to take a job aboard the S.S. *Glomar Challenger*, the Scripps Institution of Oceanography research vessel that had earlier collected data confirming the theory of continental drift, Lee wrote a lighthearted form letter to Tom's friends, explaining Tom's sudden departure.

The *Glomar Challenger*, Lee wrote, was

making its lazy way between Honolulu and Papeete, boring holes in the ocean bottom and such things. It's a two-month voyage for which Waddell is dispensing dramamine and otherwise saving lives as the ship's doctor. Then he's free for two months with pay and plenty of time to explore the South Seas and any place else that's around. Two months later, if this voyage doesn't cure him, he'll rejoin the ship in Latin America and leave it another two months afterward in some exotic port. Europe, South Africa and other places far and near are on the schedule of embarkation and debarkation—with free airfare to and from. Sounds like fun and typically Tom, doesn't it? Lots of time to loll in the sun, play the guitar and work on one or more of the three books he has in progress.

Lee ended with a little zinger: "Somewhere along the way he hopes to meet and get to know Tom Waddell."

His letters to Tom at sea were not quite so casual:

You won't want to hear it, but I'm really lost without you. My aural orifices are stretched out of shape, straining for your step on the stair, the sound of your voice. I wake up at night, and there's only my pillow where you used to be. The telephone rings at the office, but there's no "Hi!," just a low when I remember that it will never be you again. I'm sad, but I'm glad for you, Tom, because I never wanted anything but your happiness. With all my heart, I pray that you have that now, or will find it, soon and lastingly. Know always that I have loved you, to the best of my poor ability.

Tom called the relationship "a possessional, obsessional

trip," and, even when he was losing his battle with AIDS, insisted: "It was the most painful thing I ever went through in my life, except for this fucking headache." He did admit that it was an educational experience. "I learned that you can't own somebody else," he said.

Tom survived Lee Bryan and the South Seas and returned to San Francisco, ready to bury one relationship but eager to begin another, this one with Charles Louis Deaton. Charles was twelve years older than Tom and was born in Texas. Like Tom, he was a wanderer and an adventurer.

Charles left a broken home in his teens, served as a bombardier in World War II, then went to high school in Los Angeles and Menlo Junior College in Palo Alto. He was president of his class at Menlo and then pursued studies at the University of Hawaii and the University of Maryland, where he majored in literature and journalism, and wrote for the student newspaper and the literary magazine. After graduating from Maryland, where he was again president of his class, Deaton worked as a reporter at the Washington *Star*, signed up for the CIA, and went to Europe to write and edit CIA releases. He studied German literature at the University of Frankfurt.

During the late fifties, Deaton returned to the States, experienced the bohemian life while living in Greenwich Village and the corporate life while working in public relations for Standard Oil. In 1961 he married and became a father, settling into a conventional straight life until, three years later, his wife and child were killed in a car crash.

Shattered and unable to talk about his marriage for many years afterward, Deaton transferred to San Francisco, where he continued to work for Standard Oil. He then decided to change his life drastically. He studied landscaping at the University of California in Berkeley and started a landscape-architecture business. He specialized in designing private gardens—including a notable one for the Hamm's beer company—and his work was featured in magazines in the United States, France, and England.

He met Tom Waddell early in 1974, and the two soon fell in love.

December 15, 1984

You and I left Mom in San Francisco on December 10 and flew down to Tampa to visit my mother, your grandmother, whose name is Marion Jardon, and her husband Jim Mack. She has been sending you nice things, and I send her pictures. The time has arrived for them to meet you. I had put off the trip for many reasons until now.

Mom had a tough time saying goodbye to you at the airport. She will miss you terribly.

You were wonderful on the plane. You have, aside from your beauty, a quality about you that attracts everyone you meet. It is in the way you move and in your expressions. Zohn says about your charm, "We are all in deep shit," and I know what he means. You are so bright and vibrant, it is difficult to say "no" to you.

So here we are, you and me together for an entire week without any break. We are in a mobile home on a crowded piece of farmland in a retirement community on the west coast of Florida. There are no other children around, but lots of elderly people who are spending their last days in a sort of ghetto, albeit a safe and attractive ghetto. The medical business thrives off such communities, and the local institutions are generated by the need to clothe, feed and entertain the elderly. Your relatives are concentrated here—all the family members on my mother's side who once lived in New Jersey where I grew up. There is Aunt May, my mother's younger sister, who has never married and lives with another woman. She used to be my favorite aunt, and I always thought she and I would have a discussion someday about our sexuality, but she is of another generation and such a discussion has never been forthcoming. I believe she is embarrassed by my being openly gay, but I also know that she loves me and respects me. There is just no "great connection" in our relationship, no verbalized exchange about our lifestyles. Her friend Jerry is very nice, and they both took to you.

The sexual revolution, particularly the homosexual revolution, was in full swing in San Francisco during the 1970s, and while the more flamboyant flaunted and indulged their sexual preferences in public, Tom Waddell was slightly more sedate, more private. He preferred the baths.

The baths were in a sense the heart of the "erotic capitalism" that pervaded San Francisco. They sold sex. Originally they were truly steam baths, allowing naked men to mix and mingle behind thin veils of vapor. But by the mid-seventies some of the "baths" no longer had steam, saunas, or even baths. Some offered small rooms with beds and nearby showers. The worst were snake pits, the best tasteful, even elegant. Tom preferred the upscale baths, but he wasn't always choosy.

"You could get anything, do anything," he said. "You could get fucked, you could get sucked. You could just walk around until you met somebody who appealed to you, and you might chat a little bit and then say, 'Well, how'd you like to come to my room?' 'Oh, I'd like that a lot.' "

These polite courtships were often accelerated by drugs. "I'd sometimes get stoned," Tom said, "and then I'd have sex with four or five people."

Still, Tom's tastes in sex were, by the standards of the day in San Francisco, relatively mild and conventional. "I mostly like one thing," he said. "I like men's asses. I like anal intercourse. And I like when the person I'm having sex with likes the same thing. And I'm very gentle. I like to lie and play and talk and get to know the other person."

For Tom, the bathhouses provided what he called recreational sex. "I thought recreational sex was terrific," he said, "and I felt sorry for heterosexuals who didn't have a similar kind of thing."

Tom realized, to be sure, that he was jeopardizing his health in the bathhouses; he knew that he risked contracting syphilis, gonorrhea, or herpes. But while as a physician he looked for symptoms of sexually transmitted diseases in his partners, as a newly liberated gay man he felt that a dose of clap and a shot of penicillin were a small price to pay for astounding pleasure. Years later, of course, he theorized that the seeds of his AIDS, and so many others', were sown literally in the bathhouses, but in the seventies he was having too much fun to worry.

Charles Deaton was considerably more adventurous sexually. He brought home his discoveries in the bathhouses and the bars, and flaunted them in front of Tom. Both were promiscuous; everyone was promiscuous in the gay community in the seventies. "Monogamy is not something that goes well with being openly gay," Tom explained. "It might be reasonable, legitimate, acceptable, and desirable if we had grown up in a healthy environment as youngsters, where we could talk about our homosexuality and develop healthy attitudes toward sexual relationships."

By the mid-seventies, Tom was openly gay, the subject first of an article in *The Sentinel*, a gay newspaper—"1968 Olympic decathlete now jogs with Lavender U," said the story welcoming Tom to the community—then of a profile in *The Advocate*, written by Randy Shilts, who later authored the definitive book on the early days of AIDs, *And the Band Played On.*

"Despite the fact that Waddell, at 38, still has a body most men left behind in high school, you won't be hearing any stereotyped jock talk from his mustached lips," Shilts wrote in July 1976. "Not your All-American behemoth of hypermasculinity, the tall slender Waddell is more apt to talk of existentialism and social reform than god and country. He's also gay, something that he sees as neither a salient nor reproachful part of his character.

"Check off the stereotype of star turns gay and hits the lecture circuit. Far from parlaying his homosexuality into juicy honorariums, Waddell is peacefully practicing internal medicine in San Francisco. While other newly-acknowledged gay jocks go about enticing audiences to play the guess-which-jock-is-gay game, with titillating revelations about homosexuality in sports, Waddell simply says, 'I never encountered a homosexual situation the whole time I was in sports. It was permitted to go so far, camping, embracing or pretending to be nelly in a "queer joke" sort of way—but then the taboos took over.'"

The article in *The Advocate* may have opened the closet a crack, but three months later Tom came barreling out. He and Charles Deaton were featured in the "Couples" section of *People* magazine. The headline announced: TOM WADDELL AND CHARLES DEATON: "WE HAVE THE SAME PROBLEMS AS ANY OTHER COUPLE."

For a man who insisted, "I am an itinerant, and any job I take has to include travel," Tom Waddell had chosen the perfect profession. "As a physician," he said, "you carry your job on your back."

In 1974 he was offered a job that seemed ideal, that of medical director of the Life Sciences division of the Whittaker Corporation, a multinational conglomerate led by Joe Alibrandi, a businessman with a Ph.D. in thermodynamics and friends in the Middle East.

Alibrandi learned from his friends that a number of hospitals built in the region by American companies were sitting empty, going unused because they lacked staff and equipment.

He approached the royal family of Saudi Arabia and offered to provide the hospitals with the most modern equipment and the best-trained staff. The Saudis accepted Alibrandi's offer and signed contracts with Whittaker. "Billion-dollar contracts," Tom explained.

Tom liked Alibrandi, liked the challenge, and rejected an offer to be vice president of medical affairs for Kaiser Foundation International to go with Whittaker, to run the company's operations in Saudi Arabia. His training in global medicine, his experiences in the military, his athletic tours, his energy, and his presence all prepared him for the job.

The salary was surprisingly modest, roughly $40,000 a year, but, as Tom said, "I could go anywhere, do anything I wanted. I had an unlimited expense account."

Still, before he accepted, Tom sat down with Alibrandi and told him, "Joe, there's something you need to know about me. When I'm not in Saudi Arabia, I need to be in San Francisco."

"Why?" Alibrandi asked.

"To protect a relationship," Tom said.

"Oh." Alibrandi asked a logical question. "What's her name?"

"It's not a she."

Alibrandi asked the next logical question. "What's his name?"

Tom named Charles Deaton, and to his surprise Alibrandi asked, "Do you think he'd come work for us?"

Alibrandi had no difficulty with Tom's sexual orientation. He asked only that Tom do nothing to embarrass the company, and Tom readily agreed. "I never looked for or touched anyone while I was on business," he said.

When *People* magazine approached Tom about coming out in one of the world's most popular publications, he felt he had to clear the project with Alibrandi. "I'd like your permission to do this," Tom said. "I think it's important. I think we can be role models."

Alibrandi hesitated. Homosexuality was a crime in much of the Arab world; it was also practiced in much of the Arab world. The Arabs, in matters of sex, were masters of hypocrisy. Alibrandi feared that the article might offend clients and potential clients, but, reluctantly, he gave Tom permission.

The only other person Tom had to persuade was Charles Deaton. "In for a dime, in for a dollar," Deaton said. "What have we got to lose?"

The *People* article was a valentine. Barbara Walters was on the cover, Betty Ford and the Fonz on the inside. Angie Dickinson and Burt Bacharach were splitting up on one page, and Tom Waddell and Charles Deaton were declaring their love on another.

"There are lots of gays who have stable relationships," Tom was quoted as saying, "and simply do not go through the great traumas, the anonymous promiscuity, the one-night stands you always hear about."

Tom's comments were not exactly forthright. *People* heard what it wanted to hear. The magazine did not dwell on the baths; the Sisters of Perpetual Indulgence, drag nuns, did not get a mention. *People* reported that Tom and Charles had met at an art gallery and "courted in a very old-fashioned way."

The magazine did detect one difference between Tom and Charles and Ozzie and Harriet: The Nelsons were not into drugs; Tom and Charles were. "They dropped acid on Charles's theory that 'if we could weather that together, we could handle any problems a normal couple has.' "

And what was the impact of the LSD trip?

" 'Then,' laughs Tom," according to *People*, " 'we finally decided to get together in a classic moment—isn't that always the way?—over a home-cooked dinner.' "

The article continued in the same warm and reassuring tone:

"They are married—with all the traditional commitments, in their own eyes . . .

"The warm glow of *Gemütlichkeit* pervades the Waddell-Deaton household . . .

"White cats named Dome and Spike purr sleepily in separate straw baskets in the kitchen . . .

" 'Charles does most of the cooking,' Tom advises . . .

" 'You do spaghetti very well,' interjects Charles . . .

"Not unlike other newlyweds, Charles and Tom envision a dream house. . . .

" 'We've both understood how hard it would be as well as how much fun,' says Charles. 'A continuing balancing act— that is what all serious relationships are.' "

"It was so dumb," Tom said. "It could have been great." Still, for all its saccharine sentiments, Tom was glad the article had been written—pleased that he had shattered a few stereotypes, awakened a few people, and perhaps eased the pain of a few others. "I wanted them to know that it was okay to be gay, it was okay to be homosexual," he said. "You can be gay and you can be anything you want, and what difference does it make?

"The important thing was that *People* magazine was saying, 'Oh, by the way, look at these two. They are our couple of the week.' It just blew a lot of minds."

Tom was delighted to be out. "The greatest release I've ever felt," he said. "No more subterfuge. 'Where are you going?' 'I'm going to the movies.' No more lying."

He had informed many of his friends that the article was about to appear, that he was acknowledging his homosexuality publicly and didn't want them to be surprised or shocked. The reactions of his friends were almost universally positive. "I know we understand you better," Gene Waddell responded, "and with that understanding comes an even deeper kind of love for you."

"Thank God!" Jackie Leonard, the teacher of psychology told Tom. "We always knew. We thought you didn't."

Quenby Sameth, Tom's former fiancée, did not know that the article, or Tom, was coming out. "Dear Tom," she wrote:

> Bought my first copy of *People* today! Jerry [her husband] 'discovered' your name and photo in the N.Y. *Times* ad—good thing he reads the *Times* thoroughly! Of course I rushed right out to get it! I'm so proud of you—carried the magazine around all day, showing it to people—felt like a grandmother with baby pictures. I'm also very happy for you. I'm sure there's a certain amount of distortion (of emphasis) in *any* article, but if it is generally accurate, you sound pleased with your life and content, and that's wonderful.

Quenby's letter filled Tom in on her life during the decade since they last saw each other. She had undergone a radical mastectomy, then a prophylactic and cosmetic mastectomy. She had faced up to death and endured depression, and she had taken up ice-skating and become so good that she was teaching the sport. "Are you a John Curry fan?" she asked Tom. "He's a good friend—beautiful person." The British skater, Quenby said, had more or less "come out."

Then in her letter Quenby, too, came out. Through a friend, she said, "I met a lot of lesbians, started hanging out with them—didn't take me *too* long to figure out that I'm a lesbian, too! A knockout revelation—feel *whole* for the first time in my life. I don't like the term 'bi-sexual'—sounds too swingerish—and I also see it as a word implying 'one or the other.' I'm just a lesbian virgin who is also married and heterosexual."

Of all the friends and acquaintances Tom contacted before the publication of the *People* article, only one did not contact him. He did not hear a word from Bill Toomey.

December 17, 1984

Mom met us at the airport with a yellow and a red rose. You were kind of blitzed out after the trip—a long one. What a crack-up you were on the plane. Our little area (seat 16-D) looked like a hurricane had hit. You and your endless energy kept me going all the time. You were all over the place, walking on the food tray, under the seat, and in the aisle. But it was funny and charming. What a great challenge you give me—to direct all that energy in a positive way and at the same time to apply enough discipline in a loving way to make you understand the value of responsibility—you are never too young to begin to feel that.

It's good to be home again. Mom is chagrined that you are not more demonstrative toward her, but you have your own pace and are quite independent already. I can see where you will be a very strong person with strong likes and dislikes. Good!

Tom Waddell was not the first prominent gay athlete to go public. The first was a professional football player who, in his autobiography, *The David Kopay Story*, had written of his struggle with his homosexuality and of his love affair with a fellow Washington Redskin.

Kopay came out in 1975, and Tom admired his courage but not his style. Tom feared that Kopay confirmed more stereotypes than he destroyed—the sort of stereotypes that prompted too many people to irritate Tom with comments like, "Funny, you don't look gay."

More than a decade later, when the idea for this book first germinated, I called a friend, a gay activist named David Rothenberg, who had been the public-relations man for Kopay's book, and asked him if he knew how I could get in touch with Tom Waddell.

"Do you think we *all* know each other?" Rothenberg replied.

In the 1970s Tom carried on two love affairs simultaneously: one with Charles Deaton, the other with boats. In fact, he detected similarities between the two. "It's a high-maintenance relationship," he once said of his romance with Deaton, "like having a wooden boat again when what I want is fiberglass. You spend your time maintaining a wooden boat. You spend your time enjoying a fiberglass boat."

His first boat was a wooden one, a fairly modest twenty-eight-footer he named the *Windtree*. Then he bought a forty-eight-foot Grand Banks, a fiberglass boat large enough to sleep twelve. He called it the *Enge*.

The boat cost more than $100,000, but Tom had always been careful with money—hoarding his army earnings, for instance, investing them and his medical income in stocks and real estate. He was never a profligate spender, and even when he indulged himself with the Grand Banks, he calculated that by chartering the boat out he would make it pay for itself.

Tom lived for a while aboard the *Enge*, docked in Sausalito, across the bay from San Francisco. He loved to load up the boat with food and friends and Scrabble sets, anchor in a secluded cove, and party for a weekend.

Once he took the *Enge* to Oakland, and while he was at the dock, preparing the boat for charter, a group of husky young men approached him and asked if he would take them for a quick ride around the bay. Tom said he couldn't, but the men were insistent. They offered him $100. "Who are you guys?" Tom said.

"We're the New York Jets," one said.

Tom couldn't resist; he agreed to take the Jets for a tour of the bay. But as soon as they pulled away from the dock, they began stripping off their clothes, dashing around the deck, and mooning every boat that approached. Tom was stunned. "I wasn't turned on," he said. "I was terrified. I kept thinking, *The Coast Guard's going to come by. I'm going to lose my boat. I'm going to lose my ass. I'm going to lose everything.*"

The Coast Guard never did sight Tom's strange cargo—but the next day the Jets lost their football game to the Oakland Raiders.

Suellen Manning, who was working as a nurse at the University of California Medical Center, sometimes joined Tom on the *Enge*, and one weekend, after long and gentle hours together, Tom suggested they make love.

They had known each other for several years. They had worked together, played together, shared secrets and feelings, soothed each other and spurred each other on, healed each other and truly loved each other. But they had never made love. They had thought about it, talked about it, even laughed about it, but that was all. When Tom brought up the possibility of the two of them having a child, Suellen gave in, not to him, but to her insecurities. She was overweight, and she felt that she was unattractive, and Tom was beautiful.

They had one wonderful night aboard the *Enge*. They held each other for a long time, and they pleased each other.

They never made love again.

. . .

Tom had friends, gay and straight, who found it difficult to understand how he could make love, even once, to a woman, and how a straight woman could make love, even once, to him. He tried to enlighten them.

"I think anybody can get anyone sexually aroused," he once said, "if what they do is arousing. It doesn't have to be physical. You can sexualize warm feelings. And you don't have to be in love to make love. There's no threat, there's no performance anxiety. If it happens, it happens.

"To think of a person as only homosexual, or only heterosexual, is ridiculous."

One of Tom's favorite theories was that sexuality is a spectrum, not either/or, and that everyone is situated somewhere along the line; very few people are at one end or the other. James Broughton, the gay poet who spent many years with the film critic Pauline Kael, once came to dinner at Tom's home with his male lover, a young filmmaker, and when the conversation turned to Tom's idea of the spectrum of sexuality, Broughton said, "I'm not an either/or man, I'm a both/and man." Yet neither Tom nor Broughton ever thought of himself as bisexual, only as homosexual.

December 18, 1984

A long day. I visited you twice today, but you were napping the first time. Mommy bought you a potty to start training, but in your view, it simply was another place to sit.

While I was having my car fixed, and doing lots of window-shopping (which I love to do), Mom was having your ears pierced. You were wearing earrings when I came over this evening. The three of us celebrated Hannukah together, and Mom held you while you and I lit the Hannukah candles on the menorah. I gave you a large stone I had bought in Mombasa, and I gave Mom a tiger-eye necklace. You gave me an aloe vera plant with a cute little pot with my name in Hebrew letters on the side. Mom and you gave me a purple glass candle box with hummingbirds on the sides. The entire evening was fun.

My father is very sick with cancer, and I may go visit him soon. It will be difficult to be away from you, but I must go. I love my father very much and he is a good and gentle person. I want to share some things with him before he dies. I will also visit Enge and the Waddells—they are all important to me.

Zohn is being himself—he and I were passionate with each other this morning, then we each had a full day and this evening was a bit strained. We're both under great pressure. I also need to find a job soon.

Zohn is taking his friend Larry, who has AIDS and is dying, up to the redwood country north of San Francisco, and I fear they will execute some previously arranged pact to terminate Larry's misery. I am not against the idea, but it is fraught with many pitfalls, and I don't think Zohn has considered all of them. I warned him of the consequences.

Roger [Tom's tenant] and I fought over Hannah [Roger's dog] again tonight, and [Roger's roommate] Eric shuts it all out. Later Roger came to me and began crying because he felt so unloved and unneeded. He is out of a job and he is lost and lonely and feels he doesn't have anything to give to anyone, including his feelings.

I held him and asked him if he would stop punishing himself and do something that would be fun and pleasant. If he were occupied and enjoying himself, then Eric and I would be happy for him and would enjoy sharing our activities over dinner. I asked him to take the day tomorrow, put on some Christmas music and create a festive spirit in the hall for you—he loves you and brightened up at the prospect of the challenge. I think you will probably be delighted with what he does. Happy Hannukah, my sweetheart.

Tom worked for Whittaker from 1974 through 1981, and while he frequently returned to San Francisco, and to Charles Deaton, he lived for months at a time in Saudi Arabia, the Sudan, and the United Arab Emirates. "Living in Arabia was the pits," he said, "except that it was fascinating."

When a hospital was staffed and equipped, ready to be turned over to the Arabs, Tom might spend a few weeks or months directing the facility and supervising the medical operations. But the nature of his job was such that he spent more time stroking the Arabs than healing them.

Once Prince Turki bin Abdul Aziz Al Saud, who was the brother of King Fahd bin Abdul Aziz Al Saud, asked Whittaker to provide a physician to accompany him and his family on a trip to the Riviera. Prince Turki, besides being the brother and son of kings, was also the deputy minister of defense. Whittaker wanted to keep the prince happy, so Tom was asked to join the royal entourage.

He accepted the invitation. "We went to this very expensive hotel on the Riviera, the Lafayette, I think it was, and we took over half the hotel," he recalled. "The prince wanted me by his side most of the time."

The prince and his party had their own agenda. They slept all day and played all night. Mostly, they gambled. "What do you do when you really want to show people that you have money?" Tom said. "Can you imagine? *You lose it.* And you say, 'It's nothing, nothing.' I watched the prince lose millions and millions of dollars, and people would look at him and say, 'That guy must *really* be rich.' And that would make him happy. He was rich, and he was crazy, and he was stupid."

Despite the millions he left on the Riviera, Prince Turki still had more than enough to take his entourage, including his personal physician, to Hawaii and settle into a few floors at one of the Sheraton hotels. "Going out to dinner with them," Tom said, "I just wanted to slide under the table. We'd go to these expensive restaurants, and the waiter would bring a menu and they would just say, 'Fish, I want fried fish, and I want french fries,' and the food would come and they would taste it and say, 'No, this is not what I want.' "

His Royal Highness was accompanied by his beautiful wife, a commoner who was in turn accompanied by her brother, Mohammed al-Fassi. Al-Fassi achieved notoriety for building and then abandoning an horrendous house on Sunset Boulevard in Beverly Hills (neighbors toasted its demolition with glasses of champagne). The princess had the prince wrapped around her common pinkie.

"The princess loved to shop," Tom said. "She would walk into a store and there would be a whole rack of dresses, and she would look at them and say, 'I want these.' All of them. And then she would buy three hundred suitcases, and she would have everything delivered to the hotel. And her mother was with her and she would be buying like crazy, and the stores saw them coming and marked up the prices, and they didn't care, it was totally immaterial, they'd see twenty beautiful diamond rings and they'd buy them all. And then they'd fill up the suitcases and ship everything off to one of the seven or eight houses they had around the world, and they would probably just go into a storage room."

Tom was awed. "I watched them spend one million dollars one day in Honolulu."

The prince and his family did not forget Tom. They bought him a lovely lapis ring worth $200 or $300, and on the last day they were all together, the prince presented Tom with a bonus.

"He had a satchel with five million dollars in it," Tom said, "and he carried it into the bedroom with him and he said, 'One minute,' and I could hear the latches opening. I thought,

Oh, my God. Here it comes. And he took a paper bag and he began stuffing it, and then he came back to me and just dropped the paper bag in my lap and said, 'Thank you very much.' And I said, 'Thank you,' and just sat there squirming, not able to leave until he said, 'You may go.' And then I went to my room and closed the door and opened the bag and found two hundred bills inside, all twenties. A total of four thousand dollars."

For his thirty days with the royal entourage, Tom charged Whittaker $1,500 a day, a total of $45,000. "They were pissed at me," he recalled, "and I said, 'If you asked me to do this again, the price would be twenty-five hundred a day. I earned every penny of that. *You* spend a month with them and then come back and tell me I overcharged you.'"

In all fairness to the Saudis, Prince Turki bin Abdul Aziz al Saud was not highly regarded by the other Royal Highnesses in his land.

Tom considered the trip to be another learning experience. "I came over here because I wanted a cross-cultural experience, I wanted to understand the Arab culture," he told himself. "Well, this is part of the Arab culture. Who am I to get judgmental?"

December 20, 1984

Today I put you on my back and we went to Macy's and Neiman-Marcus to see the Christmas decorations. You, of course, were wide-eyed at all the trappings and the crowds. I loved being with you. You are very bright and alert. Nothing seems to escape your eye and you cannot be fooled. I apply a good deal of discipline to you, and at the same time I encourage your independence. I like your inquisitiveness, and yet there must be constraints to let you know that total freedom can be dangerous if not lethal. You are quite sensible and

well-behaved. I have the feeling that you are going to be a remarkable woman.

There is a lot of trouble in the world—that is not new
news but there are greater threats than ever before. This
country you were born in has some terrible values—based on
the profit motive and greed. It seems to consume most people. I hope we can give you a more reasonable set of values,
but it will be difficult unless you can understand the value of
history. Only through history and art can you be aware of the
meaning of your life.

Homosexuality was a crime in Saudi Arabia, but, as far as Tom
could tell, and not from firsthand experience, it was also a
necessity.

"Young Arab men," he said, "may not even see a woman
until she is of a certain age. The women are all sequestered.
They're not allowed to be seen even at school, or anywhere
else. They have their own schools, their own everything. There
is no mixing at all.

"So here are Arabs, hundreds, or thousands, or even millions of Arabs, who are buddies. And what do they do? Well,
mutual masturbation. Buggering. Almost like an English
boarding school. And it's okay, you just don't let anybody know
about it. You certainly don't indicate that you like it. It is what
I call utilitarian sex."

On the other hand, Tom liked the interaction he saw between Arab men. "You'll see them walking hand in hand," he
said. "You'll see them kissing. They're extremely affectionate,
they're very intimate, and they obviously love each other—love
each other as men. But it's verboten to have the appearance of
being sexual."

The Arab attitude toward homosexuality sometimes be-
mused him. He went to one oil-rich country and found that
the king was in fact a queen. "He was gay as a goose," Tom
said. "But it was never talked about."

His palace, Tom said, was something out of Oz.

Of course, the Arabs' attitude toward heterosexuality was hardly free of hypocrisy, either. Tom occasionally caught flights from Riyadh to Beirut, then the Las Vegas of the Middle East, and he would find himself surrounded by members of the royalty or near-royalty. The women would be very circumspect, dressed in purdah, veils, black outfits. They were not permitted to dress any other way. "If you looked them in the eye," Tom said, "they could have you thrown in jail."

When the plane took off, the women would sit quietly in their first-class seats, while their husbands, sitting behind them, would start drinking. But the moment the plane crossed the border into Lebanon, there was an amazing transformation. "Off came the purdah," Tom said. On came miniskirts and multicolored sunglasses, and out came cigarettes and liquor. "They would start drinking and smoking and carrying on like crazy whores," he said.

Tom loved Beirut, particularly the Phoenicia Hotel. The day the war began in Beirut, Tom packed his suitcase and left the Phoenicia to go to the airport and as his plane lifted off the runway, bombs were falling on the beautiful and corrupt city.

Bombs and other arms were the stock-in-trade of Adnan Khashoggi, the Saudi businessman who, like Prince Turki bin Abdul Aziz al Saud, enlisted Tom as his personal physician. Unlike the prince, Khashoggi was good company, polite, considerate, accessible.

He was also overweight. "With the kind of stress you put yourself through," Tom said, "you might have some problems later on." Khashoggi appreciated Tom's concern and counsel.

Khashoggi had just begun to build his fortune in the midseventies. He had upgraded his private plane from a DC-9 to a 737 when Tom knew him; later he moved up to a 747. He was equally at ease in a business suit or a burnoose. "He'd sit on the floor of the plane, fix himself a drink, have everyone gather around him and we'd chat," Tom recalled.

Khashoggi, who represented Whittaker in negotiations in the Middle East, once called Tom in the middle of the night in Saudi Arabia and said, "Come on, we're going to the Sudan," and they boarded his plane and took off. President Numeiri himself met them at the airport in Khartoum and whisked them off by limousine to the presidential palace. Khashoggi talked to the Sudanese president, then handed Tom a piece of paper. "Sign this," he said.

"Shouldn't I read it first?" Tom said.

"It's a two-hundred-million-dollar contract," Khashoggi said.

"Oh," said Tom, and signed the contract.

That afternoon at the airport, amid considerable fanfare, Khashoggi stood on a podium next to his plane and announced that he was delivering to President Numeiri a state-of-the-art computer, "a gift from me to you."

Tom overheard an aide whisper into Khashoggi's ear, "He doesn't have electrical power."

Khashoggi did not miss a beat. "And a generator," he said.

Khashoggi was the consummate capitalist and an arms merchant, and in principle, Tom should have been no more fond of him than he was of Lyndon Johnson or Ronald Reagan. But he was flexible. "Regardless of my political bent," he said, "I loved those experiences. There was no way I could ever duplicate them."

Tom Waddell went to the Montreal Olympics in 1976, not as a decathlete but as a doctor. He was the team physician for the Saudi Arabian team.

The year before, he had approached the Saudi Ministry of Youth Welfare and suggested that he help the agency start the first sports program in the country. The Saudis promptly put $20 million into the program, and Tom got it going.

His reward was the trip to his second Olympics, the first for Saudi athletes.

December 25, 1984

Hello, sweetness. I am writing you from Clifton, New Jersey, on Christmas Day. You were here when you were eight months old. Now I am back to help take care of my father, who is dying of cancer. It's an uncomfortable situation because my younger brother and his wife do not want me around. Dad was invited to their home for dinner today. I was not, but I wouldn't have gone, anyway; I couldn't be that much of a hypocrite. I spent the day with Enge in New York—he is just as bad off as Dad. I cooked for him, too, but neither of them has any appetite.

I spend my time with Dad and Enge talking about the past and examining our relationships and how we have grown. I cannot think of anything else they would care to do. It seems important to each of them to talk about their lives—somehow it gives them validation.

I called you and Mom today. You had the entire family with you for Xmas dinner—including Zohn, Eric and Roger. I spoke to all of them and Mom brought you to the phone long enough for me to hear that delicious laugh of yours. How I miss you, sweetheart. I came back from New York and sat down to look at the pictures of you I had brought along.

I am not sleeping well. I worry about the USOC lawsuit, and my Dad and Enge, and Zohn, and the world that you might inherit—not a very pretty place at times—but I keep my wits about me with some good reading and positive

thoughts about the future. Mom and I are talking about getting married—and of course bringing you a brother or a sister
in with the deal.

  Mom is so wonderful—you are a lucky girl.

  I love you and I miss you.

When Tom was not traveling for Whittaker, when he was
home and his relationship with Charles Deaton was still thriv-
ing, he and Charles periodically hosted Albion Evenings, concerts and performances at their home on Albion Street in the
Mission district of San Francisco.

  Their home, "Albion," was a cavernous Victorian structure
built in the late nineteenth century by the man who owned the
local Tivoli Opera House. His nickname was "Tiv," which explained the ornate wooden *T* on the front of the gable atop the
building. Around the turn of the century it had served as a
turnverein, the headquarters for a German-American social
and hiking club. The main hall housed a stage beneath tower-
ing ceilings.

  Albion stands very close to the site of the Franciscan fathers' original mission, the eighteenth-century seed of the
settlement that became San Francisco and, with the gold rush
of 1849, was transformed into a flourishing port city.

  There are unconfirmed reports that Sarah Bernhardt
appeared on the stage at Albion near the end of the nineteenth century, and it is known that Jimmy Cagney later
danced on it.

  A couple of times a month, Tom and Charles invited mu-
sicians, dancers, or poets to perform on the stage and gathered
two or three dozen friends, some from the bars and some from
the baths, to enjoy the performances, converse and eat hors
d'oeuvres, and sip wine—only white wine, to protect the white
carpets. "White wine for carpets," Eric Wilkinson suggested to
Tom, "red wine for linoleum."

  It was all very civilized, very San Francisco.

•   •   •

Eventually, just as *People* had anticipated, Tom and Charles, like so many other couples, had their problems. Tom became less accepting of Charles's weakness for bringing home other men, especially when it was, so often, the same man.

"He had to mention that fucking Billy," Tom complained after one conversation with Charles.

They argued, accused, denied, inflicted and endured pain. Tom escaped, to the sea, to drugs, to sex.

Tom had sold the *Enge* at about the same time he bought Albion, which at $125,000 was a bargain even in its run-down condition. But the sea still appealed to him, and in 1978 he answered an ad placed in the San Francisco *Chronicle* by a car dealer who wanted company sailing a forty-two-foot ketch to a convention in Hawaii. Tom was one of a half-dozen volunteers who were selected, but the voyage turned into a nightmare of bickering and battling. It was a small miracle that the boat and its mutinous crew made it to Hawaii.

The car dealer's name was also Bill.

In the late seventies Tom was often unhappy with both his personal and his professional life. When he was in the States, he supplemented his Whittaker income by working, as he had in the early seventies, in emergency rooms as close as Redding, California, and as far away as Steubenville, Ohio. "I seem to be surrounded by disease and anguish and it is affecting my work," he wrote in his diary. "I am thinking even more seriously about abandoning medicine in favor of an itinerant existence."

Another time, he wrote: "I hate this E.R., the patients, the doctors, the pollution, the mentalities. All the things in life that are cheap, mundane and valueless seem to be exemplified in what I see and hear and feel at this place."

The high of the early seventies, the thrill of coming out, in the baths and in print, the excitement of a challenging job and a new lifestyle, seemed to be giving way to a low. Tom tried acid, grass, cocaine, stimulants, and depressants—always the explorer, never the addict. He also attempted to will himself high without drugs, but was unsuccessful.

He spent much of 1979 in Britain recruiting physicians and prominent professors of medicine to visit Saudi Arabia to give lectures, share their expertise, and initiate medical programs. He lived in London a good part of the time and was delighted to discover other gay men who worked for Whittaker there.

In the spring of 1980, as he and Charles drifted farther apart, he found himself back in the baths, again seeking out recreational sex, again paying his dues to erotic capitalism. "What does one want after spending the better part of five hours stoned and screwing as though tomorrow begins a new life of celibacy?" he asked himself in one diary entry. "It was too much, of course, but one never seems to know when too much sex is enough!"

A few weeks later he noted: "Too many sex trips these days—seems like a different one every night lately, and I can't even keep them sorted out."

Then, in the middle of 1981, he accepted his final assignment for Whittaker. He agreed to be a marketing agent in Dubai, away from Charles, and from sex. He saw homosexuality around him, but he wasn't even slightly tempted. "It was of the Arabian variety," he said. "Not the least bit intimate, and dangerous if one didn't know the nuances of getting together."

His head began to clear. He enjoyed celibacy and solitude. "I wanted to feel I could exist alone," he recalled, "outside of addictive relationships, away from the overwhelming emphasis on sexuality in the gay life in San Francisco." He smoked hash, listened to music, wrote snippets of short stories, and scribbled down notes for a novel.

He informed Joe Alibrandi, his boss and friend, that he had decided to leave Whittaker, that he intended to become a writer. Alibrandi was understanding, and generous. He told Tom that Whittaker would keep him on a retainer. In a sense, Tom was back on scholarship again.

December 29, 1984

I've been caring for my Dad (I'll call him "Grandpa" from now on) and Enge. Today I left Grandpa in my brother's care and came into the city to get Enge and his cousin Sophie. We are all very close and are perhaps more of a family than my real family was. Enge lives in a project apartment on West 17th Street—it's on the 23rd floor of a building that sits not far from the Empire State Building (which is where Grandpa Waddell once did his acrobatics on the top ledge in 1935). Enge is crotchety and demanding, self-centered and confused, but he has always been there for me—supportive in so many ways. In fact, even now, when he is so sick and old, the easiest way to divert him from his complaints is to tell him that I am in trouble. Occasionally, when I am tired, I use that ploy, but I really don't want him doing things for me anymore. I need to do more for him.

Sophie is about 92 and while walking her to the car and talking to her, I asked, "How have you been?" She said, "Well, I'm blind and deaf and can't walk, but other than that I'm okay!" What a character. We went to South Nyack, where Mom and I had taken you in April of this year. Mary, Enge's sister-in-law, had a dinner for us all. I love Mary—she is a great woman and I wish you could know her better. I had sent her pictures of you, Mom and me last week.

Danny Menaker, her son; Catherine, Danny's wife; and

Willy, their son, were also there. You met them in April at the farm house in Massachusetts when we visited Enge. Danny is very competitive with Willy, he always wants him to say and do things to show how bright he is. Willy is a few weeks older than you, but you are taller. Perhaps you'll be friends some day. At least we'll have some interesting photographs for the two of you to laugh about.

Back in New York, Enge and I talked about Drew Pearson, the famous columnist whom Enge was close to and I had met and then taken care of when he got sick in Washington, D.C., in 1969.

My father is very bad, and Enge is very old. They both need constant attention, and I am providing that for the nonce. But I am also missing you and I don't think I can stay away much longer.

Your Mom and I want to get married in January and then give you a little sister or brother—our family will grow and we will have a wonderful life. I must get back to you soon. I love you.

In June 1980, between assignments for Whittaker, Tom happened to be watching television one day with a friend named Mark Brown, the sports editor of the Bay Area *Reporter*. Flipping among the channels, Tom came upon an event called the Gay Men's Bowling Tournament.

The competitors were strong and skillful athletes, clearly bowlers first and gay second. Too often, Tom felt, the gay community was represented in public only by its most outrageous elements, by drag queens and leather boys, who were, in his view, only a small percentage of the community.

The majority of gay men, Tom knew, were, like himself, professionals, doctors, lawyers, advertising men, salesmen, men who went to the theater and the cinema, who voted and ate out, bowled and played softball and rooted for the 49ers. They were not flamboyantly lusting for attention.

Tom was convinced that too much attention, from both the gay community and the straight, focused on the gay ghetto and on young white males, and excluded women and blacks and the aging. To too many people, Tom said, "Gay rights was, 'You can't stop me from getting a blow job on Castro Street.'"

That sort of thinking, Tom felt, promoted stereotypes. He wanted to destroy them. He wanted to emphasize that gay men were *men*, not that they were *gay*, and that lesbian women were *women*, not that they were *lesbians*. He didn't want them to lose their homosexual identity, or hide it; he just didn't want them to be dominated by it, pigeonholed by it.

The Gay Men's Bowling Tournament struck Tom as a step in the right direction. He and Mark Brown began to envision an athletic competition that would go even further—a festival modeled on the ancient Olympics but modified, open to everyone regardless of age or race or gender or sexual orientation, or even ability.

Tom, Mark Brown, and Paul Mart held the first meeting of the United States Gay Olympic Committee on June 15, 1980. Mart was a short, wiry contradiction of homosexual stereotypes. He was a former movie stuntman who had served as a stand-in for the quintessential tough guy, Jimmy Cagney. He was also a member of the Rodeo Cowboys Hall of Fame.

For a year the Gay Olympics was an idea, a dream, nothing more. But when Tom Waddell finished his tour for Whittaker the idea, the dream, began to consume him.

In the summer of 1981 he and Eric Wilkinson and Roger Tubb drove across the country and, armed with a guide to gay bars and baths, stopped in major cities to test the waters— literally and figuratively—to see if the Gay Olympics were feasible, to see if the idea appealed to gay men and lesbian women. Tom had little difficulty finding gay men who were eager to speak with him. He talked, and Eric and Roger distributed leaflets.

Tom was encouraged by the reactions he encountered and began to plan for the first Gay Olympic Games to be held in 1982 in San Francisco, the Olympia of homosexuality. "This event is becoming an important opportunity for gay men and women all over the world to demonstrate that our character has a wide and varied range," he wrote to prospective supporters of the Games. "It is an opportunity to expand beyond a falsely tainted image. It is an opportunity to show that gay men and women, like all other responsible citizens of the United States, participate in the same ideal."

He squeezed visits to Enge and to the Waddells into his cross-country trip with Eric and Roger. Enge was well into his eighties, perhaps pleased to see his protégé back at The Farm but certainly not to entertain the protégé's friends. "Tom kept apologizing for Enge," Eric Wilkinson remembered.

The original three-man committee evolved into San Francisco Arts & Athletics Inc., and Tom became chairman of the board in fact as well as title. He took a course in the delicate, and essential, art of fund-raising, and absorbed the lessons well: Explain the philosophy behind the Games, ask for money, and then keep your mouth shut. If the prospective donor speaks next, he'll give; if you speak, he won't.

Tom tested the theory on a friend named Bill Kraft. He explained the egalitarian nature of the Games, then he outlined the financial needs. "Now that you're acquainted with the Gay Olympics, and I think you have a grasp of it," Tom said, "I'd like to request that you make a donation of five thousand dollars."

Tom shut up.

Bill Kraft spoke up, and wrote out a check for $5,000.

Tom was ecstatic to discover that the technique he had been taught was effective. "Bill Kraft was so pissed," Tom said. "He called me the following day and yelled and yelled and yelled."

Tom weakened and offered to give Kraft his money back. "You do what you want," Kraft said.

Tom deposited the check and wrote Kraft a thank-you note.

The Games began to take shape, a blend of events artistic and athletic, concerts and exhibitions, as well as competitions. San Francisco Arts and Athletics chose the dates of August 28 to September 5, 1982, and the mayor of San Francisco, Dianne Feinstein, said she would designate the nine-day period "Gay Olympic Games Week." The city promised Kezar Stadium, once the home of the 49ers, for the opening and closing ceremonies.

A computer whiz with a musical bent offered to compose a Gay Olympic anthem that would synthesize elements of all the world's national anthems. The offer was politely turned down. But a gay torch run was set up, like the quadrennial run from Mount Olympus. This one would start at an historic homosexual landmark, the Stonewall Inn in New York, and finish in San Francisco, ending with the igniting of the flame by Susan McGreivey and George Frenn, both committed to the Gay Olympics and both, like Tom, former competitors in the straight Olympics. McGreivey, as Susan "Dougie" Grey, swam for the United States in the 1956 Games in Melbourne; Frenn threw the hammer in Mexico City and in Munich.

All the pieces fell into place—commitments to produce the commemorative pins, T-shirts, and posters that validate every major sporting event; a fairly haphazard lineup of fourteen sports, each open to both men and women, except wrestling, which was limited to males, and rugby, which, despite or perhaps because of its ruggedness, was limited to females; team trials in gay communities across the country and around the world, even though the Gay Olympics were, in theory and practice, open to all who wished to enter.

In Holland, the twenty-five members of the Dutch soccer team earned the money for their trip to San Francisco by cutting and selling a record called "The Ball," which shot up to number ten on the Netherlands hit parade. The record was so profitable that the soccer team was able to bring along sixty members of its fan club.

Elton John, Bette Midler, and Jane Fonda were invited to participate in the festivities, and none of them accepted. But Tina Turner did. She said she would sing at the opening ceremonies.

The straight world, its press and public, tended to ignore the Games, and segments of the gay community tried to. Some gays and lesbians lacked both confidence and pride in their athletic abilities and worried that a public demonstration of their perceived inadequacies would be embarrassing, even painful. Others feared gay-bashing or other violent reactions to the Games.

Tom strove to calm those fears. In a newsletter promoting the competition, he argued that violence toward gays occurred because they were not "viewed as fully vested citizens, but rather like marginal beings who can be transgressed and maligned without thought of recrimination. Even worse, or as bad, is the common view that gay men are sissies and therefore 'weaklings.' "

In his enthusiasm, Tom occasionally stumbled. For one fund-raiser, for instance, he decided to screen *Olympia*, Leni Riefenstahl's beautiful but controversial documentary about the 1936 Olympic Games in Berlin, which were presided over by her benefactor and chancellor, Adolf Hitler. Riefenstahl

had earlier made *Triumph of the Will*, a more blatant ode to
Nazism. Artistically, Tom's decision was an intelligent one. Politically, though, it was stupid.

SUPPORT GAY OLYMPICS NOT NAZI PROPA-
GANDA FILMS, urged leaflets that were distributed by
Jewish gays and lesbians, many of them members of Sha'ar
Zahav, San Francisco's gay synagogue. Tom was rankled, but
he was a realist, and he knew his cause would be severely
weakened without the support of the Jewish gay community.
He canceled the showing of *Olympia*.

"I feel I'm yielding to the same kind of censorship the Nazis themselves practiced," he complained to the journalist
Randy Shilts. His remark, luckily, caused no further damage.

But he then faced a much greater problem. On December
26, 1981, eight months before the opening ceremonies, he
wrote a letter to the executive director of the U.S. Olympic
Committee, Colonel F. Don Miller. In 1968, as the liaison between the USOC and its contingent of military athletes, it had
been Miller who had threatened Tom with court-martial for
his statements supporting Tommie Smith and John Carlos.

> When we originally filed our articles of incorporation in
> Sacramento, California, we were told we could not use
> the name "Olympic" in our corporate name or logo. We
> thus became "San Francisco Arts & Athletics . . ."
>
> We recently heard indirectly that we could not even
> call our athletic contests the "Gay Olympic Games," at
> least not without permission from the United States
> Olympic Committee. . . .
>
> [We] were only aware of the word "Olympic" as a
> generic term, referring to an event that predated
> Christ. . . . [We] were also aware that there were "Arm-
> chair Olympics," "Special Olympics," "Handicapped
> Olympics," "Police Olympics," even "Dog Olympics."

There are also 33 listings in the San Francisco phone book using the term "Olympic."

Col. Miller, these games are very specialized indeed. Our outreach and emphasis differs widely from the traditional Olympic Games in that we, openly gay people around the world, are struggling to produce an image that more closely resembles the facts rather than some libidinous stereotype generated over decades of misunderstanding and intolerance. . . .

Some things are changing. Homosexuality is not something that needs to be "understood," any more than one's tastes in food can be understood; it is simply something that needs to be accepted.

We feel strongly that the term "Olympic" is integral to what we intend to achieve. Our eight days of cultural events and sport will be a testament to our character and our wholesomeness; arts and athletics within the ancient Olympic format.

If permission, according to law, is a necessity, then we hereby apply for such, and assume that you will be fair in view of the precedents already set. We, in turn, will demonstrate our gratitude in ample ways as the 1984 Olympic Games in Los Angeles draw closer.

Copies of the letter, signed by Tom as the chairman of SFAA, were sent to Senator Alan Cranston, Governor Jerry Brown, Mayor Dianne Feinstein, and the San Francisco Board of Supervisors.

The law to which Tom referred was the Amateur Sports Act of 1978 (Public Law 95-606), passed on November 8, 1978, which states:

Without the consent of the Corporation [the USOC], any person who uses for the purpose of trade, to induce the sale of any goods or services, or to promote any theatrical exhibition, athletic performance or competition—

(1) the symbol of the International Olympic Committee, consisting of interlocking rings;

(2) the emblem of the Corporation, consisting of an escutcheon having a blue chief and vertically extending red and white bars on the base with 5 interlocking rings displayed on the chief;

(3) any trademark, trade name, sign, symbol or insignia falsely representing association with, or authorization by, the International Olympic Committee or the Corporation; or

(4) the words "Olympic," "Olympiad," "Citius Altius Fortius [the Olympic motto]," or any combination or simulation thereof tending to cause confusion, to cause mistake, to deceive, or to falsely suggest a connection with the Corporation or any Olympic activity;

shall be subject to suit in a civil action by the Corporation. . . .

Miller informed Tom that the law was the law, that San Francisco Arts & Athletics (SFAA) could not use the word "Olympic" in any way. "The position of the United States Olympic Committee has nothing to do with the issue of homosexuality," Miller insisted. "Rather, it has to do with the rights vested in the United States Olympic Committee through Public Law. . . . To allow your organization to make use of such terminology would dilute [its] meaning and significance. . . ."

December 31, 1984

I am in Clifton with Grandpa. He started off well today, but got worse as the day went on. I did laundry, shopped for his birthday (January 2) and cooked, but he had more pain as the day progressed. I manipulated some of his medications, but I am uneasy when it comes to treating those I love. It's so much more difficult to be objective. I am giving him a picture of you and me for his birthday.

I called everyone tonight to wish all a happy and healthy New Year. I spoke with Mom and she put you near the phone—you were making those wonderful singing sounds which delight me. I wished with all my heart that I could hold you just for a moment and have you sink your head against my neck—that's one of the most satisfying things in the world.

I am reading "Dune" and find it inspiring. It has helped me make some resolutions for 1985—stop smoking, do more writing, practice mental techniques for inner peace and sharpen my leadership devoid of ego. You are so much a part of my plans. If not for you, I would leave San Francisco and live in Europe and write—but you are the most important part of my life now and I intend to see that you grow up with all kinds of wonderful influences. I can hardly wait to see you, sweetheart.

The Gay Olympics provided Tom with an avocation, a cause, an obsession—and with the last two loves of his life, besides his daughter, Sara Lewinstein and Zohn Artman. Sara was among the earliest group of women to give her support to the Games.

Tom felt it was essential to have women involved in the project. He thought that for too long gay men and lesbian women had been at odds, wary of each other, rejected by each other even as casual friends, let alone intimate ones. Some gay men seemed to dislike every woman except Judy Garland. Some lesbian women made no exceptions. Tom envisioned the Games bringing them together.

Sara's motivation may not have been quite the same. She didn't have much use for men. She had friends who had been abused physically, and she felt she had been abused financially. But she loved sports, and she loved the idea that female athletes, especially lesbian athletes, should be recognized, encouraged, and rewarded. She had been a professional bowler, playing the West Coast tour for a few years; her restaurant, Artemis, sponsored a championship women's softball team.

Sara was the daughter of survivors of the Holocaust, Polish Jews who fled from the Warsaw Ghetto. Her father, Nathan, the grandson of a prominent rabbi, joined the underground; her mother, Hela Feldbrum, was sheltered by nuns in a convent. Both of them eluded the Nazis but not the Russians. They met in Siberia, then made their way together to Germany, Palestine, and Canada. Sara's oldest brother was born in Russia; she was born in Montreal in 1954. She was only eleven when her father, after moving his family to Los Angeles, died of cancer. She was twenty-seven when she met Tom Waddell.

"Sara and I met at the Games office," Tom said. "She walked in one day and I liked her instantly, and she liked me instantly."

Soon she came to trust Tom, too, to recognize that his concern for women was real. "Tom was a feminist from the word go," Sara said. "He reminded me of me, except that he was a man."

As the chairman of SFAA, Tom issued an invitation to the lesbian community:

WOMEN! COME FORWARD!

The Greatest Gay Woman Athlete in the World will be crowned at the Games. She will be the winner of the women's pentathlon. It's a two-day event. . . . Doesn't matter if you have no experience, we'll coach and train you. . . .

Don't worry about being too old, too young, too out of shape or too inexperienced for these Games, we're all in the same boat. If you are really not interested in being a participant down on the field, then consider participating on another level. We need all kinds of help . . . from heading a committee to stuffing envelopes. . . .

Sara and Tom stuffed envelopes, attended meetings, recruited athletes and contributors. "She worked her butt off, really worked her butt off," he said. The better they got to know each other, the more each of them thought about the possibility of having a child with the other.

One night they were driving home from a fund-raising party. "What are your thoughts about children?" Sara asked.

"Oh, I'm going to have a child someday," Tom said. "I just haven't met the right person yet."

"I think you have," said Sara.

Tom met Zohn Artman in March 1982. Zohn was the director of publicity for Bill Graham, the rock impresario, the man behind the Fillmore and Fillmore East and The Grateful Dead. Zohn knew how to put together major events, understood budgets, crowd control, and public relations, along with all the small but significant details. He had no interest in sports or the Gay Games, however, and when he was asked if he would meet Tom Waddell and perhaps counsel him, Zohn agreed reluctantly. He said he could spare Tom an hour.

When Tom arrived at his home, Zohn asked to see his budget. Tom didn't have one. What about your case statement, your outline of what you propose to do? No case statement, either. Zohn Artman felt Tom was wasting his time.

"You mean to tell me," he said to Tom, "that you are coming to people like me and asking for our time and our money, and you don't have anything in writing? It's now March, and the Games are in August?"

Zohn had no sympathy for Tom. "I walked him to the door and said 'Goodbye,'" Zohn said.

Afterward Zohn felt he might have been too harsh, so he asked a friend of his, an accomplished administrator, to help Tom prepare a budget. Ten days later Tom called upon Zohn again, equipped this time with a budget and a statement of purpose.

Zohn was impressed and said so. "Can I take you to dinner?" said Tom.

"Sure," said Zohn.

Tom suddenly leaned over and kissed him. Zohn was stunned.

"W-what m-made m-me do that?" Tom stammered. "How can I apologize?"

"Just do it again," said Zohn.

They became friends and lovers. Zohn was impressed by Tom's integrity, and by his persistence. "He's like a pit bull," Zohn said. "He gets his teeth into something and he wills it into happening." Zohn, smaller than Tom, and wiry, liked to think of himself as a pit bull, too. He threw himself into publicizing the Games and raising funds.

The executive board of SFAA set up offices on Castro Street, and dozens of people gave time and energy to the Games, securing sites for the various sports, finding housing for visiting athletes, working out a schedule of events, a system of accreditation. Tom had a hand in everything, and also managed to help coach the San Francisco track, wrestling, and soccer teams.

The war over the word *Olympic* continued, both sides bringing in legal weapons, a high-paid attorney for the Olympic Committee, a pro bono counselor for Arts & Athletics, each citing precedent to support its position.

Bill Mandel, the columnist for the San Francisco *Examiner*, did not think much of the USOC's case:

Vaughan Walker, a local attorney for USOC, yesterday advanced two reasons the committee objected to the Gay Games' use of its term. First, he told me, was the possible public misconception that the quadrennial Olympics discriminated against gays.

"The existence of separate Gay Games implies that gay people must set up their own events to avoid discrimination at the major Olympics," he said. "The Olympics do not discriminate."

Later, he said the USOC was concerned the Gay Olympics would be misperceived by the public as a sanctioned USOC event.

See—the Gay Games are either too separate from or too much like the major Olympics. Pause to scratch head over pretzel logic.

Sports Illustrated also mocked the USOC. *SI* pointed out that "the ancient Olympics, an all-male event in which participants competed in the nude, was staged by a society in which homosexuality flourished." The magazine mentioned that the Alcoholic Olympics in Los Angeles and the Pastalympics in North Dakota seemed to have escaped the USOC's ire. "We've also come across the Rat Olympics, the Crab Cooking Olympics, the Xerox Olympics, and the Armenian Olympics," Tom was quoted as saying. "The bottom line is that if I'm a rat, a crab, a copying machine, or an Armenian I can have my own Olympics. If I'm gay, I can't."

The bottom line in the *SI* article was equally acerbic: The International Olympic Committee "recently protested to the USOC what it considered the illegitimate use of the Olympic ring symbol in ads and articles in the USOC magazine, *The Olympian* . . . which makes it slightly awkward for the USOC to be screaming foul about the Gay Olympics."

While Mary Dunlap, the lawyer for SFAA, and Richard Kline, the attorney for the USOC in Washington, argued law and logic through the mails, the opening of the Games approached, and neither side went to court.

"Maybe the USOC has decided, wisely, that every knock is a boost [for SFAA] in this case," columnist Art Rosenbaum wrote in the San Francisco *Chronicle*. "Maybe the USOC expects this annoying little gadfly to die a natural death."

Not exactly. Nineteen days before the Games were to begin, the USOC obtained a federal court order restraining SFAA from using the term *Olympic* in any way.

"They were busy scratching the word 'Olympics' off thousands of tickets at the Gay Olympics office yesterday," Bill Mandel said in his next column. "The word was also coming off medals, flags, banners, posters and T-shirts.

"The Games' large ad in Sunday's Datebook will refer to them as the Gay Bleep Games. . . .

"The Olympic Committee's timing was cruel. . . ."

Tom Waddell thought it was worse than cruel.

Dear Members of the U.S. Olympic Committee:

When the USOC demeaned itself by a last-minute legal action banning our use of the word *Olympic* . . . considerable injury was inflicted on these Games, the fine athletes involved, and the Olympic ideals that inspire them. As a well-executed legalistic attack designed to insure maximum damage, your last-minute action clearly succeeded: We lost some $30,000. . . . Many people planning to attend were given the impression that the event itself had been cancelled. Finally, once again millions of ordinary people were given the message of bigotry: that there is something essentially bad and disreputable about Lesbians and Gay men and our community. . . .

As former U.S. Olympic athletes, we have represented this nation as members of the Olympic team. . . . All of us

have also spent years working in the U.S. Olympic develop-
ment effort, with a special commitment to encourage . . . full
participation for all Americans. We may seem somewhat in-
significant to some of the sports politicians and bureaucrats
who often dominate the USOC . . . but we are the kinds of
people who . . . make the Olympic movement represent the
American people, rather than merely the sports establish-
ment. We strongly doubt that the heterosexual majority of
dedicated folks we have worked with over the years in Olympic sports really support the sort of mean-spirited and petty
politics perpetrated by this appalling USOC action. . . .

American sport . . . embodies some . . . principles that
should rightly remain above political posturing. Among these
are old ideas about honor, integrity and especially fair play.
We find your transparent denials that issues of "homosexuality" are involved in your actions to be at once a glaring hypocrisy and a grave violation of the ideals you are supposed
to safeguard and promote. . . .

It is quite true that you have hurt us, and damaged these
Games with a well-timed legal assault. . . . Yet in doing so, it
is not this group of athletes, but you . . . who have cheapened
and debased the honorable word *Olympic*.
In the name of sport and fair play,

Tom Waddell, M.D.
United States Olympic team, 1968
(Track and Field: Decathlon)
Susan McGreivey (Susan "Dougie" Grey)
United States Olympic team, 1956
(Swimming)
George Frenn
United States Olympic team, 1968 & 1972
(Track and Field: Hammer throw)
Bill Paul, Ed.D.
United States Olympic team, 1964
(Judo: Heavyweight alternate)

The Gay ~~Olympic~~ Games went on.

TRIUMPH IN LONG RACE FOR RIGHTS
"Olympics" or not, many see event as
symbolic of gays' gains
By Stephanie Salter
Examiner staff writer

An estimated 10,000 spectators and 1,300 athletes from countries as diverse as Ireland and Peru cheered longest and loudest during opening day ceremonies when a pair of politicians defiantly announced "The Gay Olympic Games."

The predominantly homosexual international athletic competition, which lost its right in a court of appeals earlier this week to use the word "Olympics," held its colorful ceremonies in Kezar Stadium yesterday minus the term that has come to signify such events. . . .

But U.S. Congressman Philip Burton and San Francisco Supervisor Doris Ward paid no heed to the court of appeals, both emphatically proclaiming the games "Olympics."

The crowd for the opening ceremonies was considerably smaller than Tom had hoped for and anticipated, but it was enthusiastic, cheering the parading athletes from twelve countries and twenty-eight states, the baton twirlers, the country-and-western dancers, the songs of Tina Turner, and the jabs of mistress of ceremonies Rita Mae Brown. "Darlin'," said the author of *Rubyfruit Jungle*, the lesbian coming-of-age classic, "the only people who are queer are the people who don't love anybody."

"I've waited all my life for this," said a sixty-seven-year-old spectator, Bill Vocke. "I was born in a closet. I was in business in San Francisco for thirty-two years, and I led a double life. I'm not afraid anymore."

"The point of the Games is not so much to celebrate homosexuality," Rita Mae Brown said, "but to celebrate and affirm individual freedom."

More than 250 journalists covered the opening, including one from Germany's *Der Spiegel*. "It really attracted our attention," said Rolf Kunkel, "when the USOC asked them to drop the 'Olympics' from their name."

Tom marched in the opening parade, one hand holding Sara's and the other Zohn's.

The Games were—given the general consensus that they would be lucky to break even—a surprising success financially. They cost a modest $380,000 to stage, and they brought in $395,000. Tom was a winner on the field, too, taking the gold medal in the discus.

But his victory didn't mean nearly as much to him as the performance of a forty-four-year-old grandmother who had never before competed in an athletic event of any kind. Her children watched her finish first in a swimming race, and when Tom slipped the gold medal over her head, he was crying, she was crying, and everyone in the stands was crying.

Tom said he would never forget that, nor the sight of the early finishers in a long-distance freestyle race climbing out of the pool and hurrying to the sides to cheer on the swimmers who had not yet completed their laps.

At the closing ceremonies, SFAA announced that the Games would be held again in 1986, probably in San Francisco, and that the fight to use the "O-word" would continue.

January 1, 1985

It is the New Year, my darling. I am sleeping on the floor in the living room of my father's home. He is in his room, sleeping and dying. I have been reading for hours and now I hear firecrackers and sirens and people screaming, dogs wailing. It is past midnight. I have smoked my last cigarette.

This new year will be an important one. I expect many battles and I suspect a number of victories. I must be careful and wise to see it through. Much is at stake.

I suspect there will be several deaths—my father, Enge— possibly even mine. But I have always been an optimist and I will use that optimism as a tool and a crutch. Our world is degenerating because of low thinking and greed, but the challenge is to raise consciousness and elevate the lowest common denominator.

This will be a year when I make an attempt to teach as I've never done before.

You will be a source of inspiration to me, sweet daughter. Let us have at it. I love you.

With Gay Games I behind them, secure in their mutual respect and admiration and affection, Tom Waddell and Sara Lewinstein set out to conceive a child. Zohn Artman insisted that they use his bedroom. He decorated it like a bridal suite, which did not demand too much redecorating, and he placed a brass cradle next to the bed, a cradle that had been passed down from Mick Jagger's child to Bill Graham's child to Zohn. The setting was magnificent, the pressure enormous. Sara expected Zohn to burst in cheering at any moment. But nothing happened worth cheering about.

In early November, Tom and Sara decided to try again. They spent a weekend together in Los Angeles at the home of Sara's brother. On November 8, 1982, in a remarkable burst of pride and self-confidence, Tom wrote in his journal:

My dearest child, I think of you a great deal already.

Your mother . . . and I spent the last three nights together, in an attempt to conceive you . . . we were both
anxious about it. We are great friends and . . . I was
aware that I loved her, exclusive of our friendship and
our plans to produce you.

She is a wonderful woman with a great deal of love
and humor. She's independent and honest and fair and
sensitive. She's also very beautiful and loved by a great
many people, men and women.

Nine months and three weeks later, Sara delivered Jessica.

In the years between Gay Games I and Gay Games II, Tom
Waddell contrived to keep busy, helping to raise a daughter,
nurturing his love for Sara and Zohn, planning a bigger and
better Games, writing columns for the Bay Area *Reporter*, the
California *Voice* and *Coming Up!*, serving on the board of di-
rectors of the Northern California chapter of the American
Civil Liberties Union, acting as medical consultant to the San
Francisco Police Department, and as chief physician at the
Central Aid Station of the San Francisco Department of
Health.

But if these were crowded days for Tom, they were also
threatening days—for him, and for his friends. The gay community of San Francisco, and of the world, was becoming
aware of a mysterious and terrifying disease that, in its infancy,
was known as the gay cancer.

Newspaper stories began to appear in July 1981, small
items about scattered cases of Kaposi's sarcoma, or KS, a rare
and relatively minor form of skin cancer found previously only
in elderly Mediterranean men. There were perhaps a dozen
instances in New York, maybe half a dozen in San Francisco,
a few in Los Angeles, seemingly unconnected at first. But soon

a pattern emerged, puzzling and then chilling. The cancer was more severe than usual in cases of KS, and the patients were often young and invariably gay.

And if the unexplained spread of KS wasn't frightening enough, the Centers for Disease Control in Atlanta observed almost simultaneously a surge in occurrences of *Pneumocystis carinii* pneumonia, or PCP, a lung infection that was also attacking gay men.

KS and PCP had something more in common, at least in theory. They were diseases caused by agents that were normally repelled, or destroyed, by healthy immune systems. A growing number of gay men apparently had weakened, almost nonexistent immune systems, leaving them susceptible to virulent strains of rare diseases. Some came down with toxoplasmosis, a brain infection more commonly seen in cats. One patient died of a disease that had only been seen in sheep.

Clearly, an epidemic had struck. By 1982, KS and PCP were linked by a new acronym, GRID—gay related immune deficiency. Researchers from the Centers for Disease Control tracked down GRID patients and questioned them, asking them about their travels and their diets and their sexual histories, and, rapidly, the researchers found a common thread. He was an Air Canada flight attendant named Gaetan Dugas, a handsome and boyish blond who would walk into gay bars from Paris to San Francisco and announce, "I am the prettiest one," and rarely get an argument. Everyone loved Gaetan, and almost everyone made love with him. He claimed to have had 250 different partners a year for ten years.

By July 1982, a month before Gay Games I began, at least 40 of the first 248 men to be diagnosed with GRID—men from ten different cities—had been linked sexually to Dugas. They had all had sex with him or with someone who had had sex with him. The chances of this being a coincidence were, mathematically, zero. Gaetan Dugas became known, first in medical circles, then in the gay community, as Patient Zero.

By the time Dugas died in March 1984, when his kidneys failed after years of resisting KS and PCP and other infections, researchers had isolated the virus that caused what was by then known as AIDS—HIV, the human immunodeficiency virus. The virus, they estimated, had an incubation period of perhaps as long as ten years.

The death toll from AIDS was up to 1,500, the number of cases approaching 5,000. No longer did gays have a monopoly on the disease. Intravenous drug users, recipients of blood transfusions, their wives and girlfriends and infant children, gays and straights, all were susceptible.

No one could even guess how many thousands, or tens or hundreds of thousands, were incubating the disease and would become HIV-positive.

A specialist in infectious diseases and an expert in global medicine, Tom began writing about AIDS early in 1983 in his column, "Within Reason," in the California *Voice*. His five-part series began, **AIDS PART I: THE ECOLOGY OF DISEASE.** He quoted Dr. Jacques May's definition of disease as "that alteration of the human tissues that jeopardizes survival in their environment," and went on to talk about man's physiological response to his environment—aboriginal Peruvians, for instance, living at great altitudes developing barrel chests to help them breathe the thinner air, and Africans threatened by malaria developing sickle-cell anemia because sickled cells were immune to malarial parasites. "In each group," Tom wrote, "survival meant coming to terms with an ecological system."

Eventually Tom came to the specific subject of AIDS; he was working with the sketchiest of information, at the dawn of understanding of the disease.

Unquestionably, something has disturbed the status quo of our eco-system. It is premature to insist on pinpointing what has changed because there is too little information at present, but we can be fairly certain that within the gay population the prevalence cannot simply be attributed to "lifestyle." That is more a moral conclusion than a scientific one. We are not living differently in the past two years than we were four years ago. Something new has been added or there has been a coalescence of factors that have, by chance, found a weakness in our biological defense system.

In **AIDS PART II: EPIDEMIOLOGY**, Tom traced and praised the work of the Centers for Disease Control, then concluded:

In the gay community there is a lot of panic. Irrational statements are made about AIDS and those who have it. I have heard some real horror stories such as: someone with AIDS being asked to leave a Castro restaurant, an acquaintance who refused to eat a piece of cheese because it was cut by someone who has AIDS, and some people who have AIDS are being evicted, turned away and avoided by friends and lovers. Even people who are having rather mundane infections are being accused of having AIDS and treated like lepers.

Such fears need to be met with reason. We are an extended family and our members need support and understanding, not scorn. Science is on our side. It may tell us not to kiss so indiscriminately; it may tell us to monitor our health more carefully; but it also encourages us to consider what is sensible and what is folly.

Let us make an assumption: AIDS may possibly be transmitted through INTIMATE contact. That is also true of hepatitis and syphilis, but there is no need to avoid someone who has any of the above; simply be judicious. In fact, there is some indication that persons who have AIDS may no longer be infectious, the contagion may actually occur before the problem is manifest.

Being careful does not mean being cruel. Remember that depression, isolation and fear contribute to a person's demise and ultimately may affect the immune system further. We need to contribute to the well-being of those who have AIDS because to do less is to MAKE them victims.

Tom's words were calm, rational, and cautious, blending facts and theories and supposition. He was offering sensible counsel at a time when hardly anyone else did.

Later in the series, Tom sounded a clear warning:

OF THE TOTAL CASES UP TO NOVEM-BER 12, 1982, 73 PER CENT OF THE DIAGNOSED CASES OCCURRED AMONG HOMOSEXUAL OR BISEXUAL MEN. There is something unique among us that creates a greater risk than to most other people and I feel it is not a single factor. Surely, there are many non-gays who have most of the same risk factors as our gay brothers . . . genetic predisposition, nutritional habits, multiple sex partners, use of recreational drugs, stress, anxiety, fatigue and so on and so on. But there are undeniable differences as well. We are exposed to sperm and fecal matter in amounts and ways that non-gays aren't. We use a great deal more nitrites. We have a higher incidence of hepatitis-B, cytomegalovirus and intestinal parasites. . . .

. . . Perhaps we have been excessive, and that is not a moral judgment; it is a scientific one. We have probed a particular theme in our lives which we call sexual freedom (is there really such a thing?) and have crossed some natural border.

Our sexual practices are a manifestation of natural drives, but like other natural drives such as the need to eat, to explore other levels of consciousness through drugs and alcohol, there is a point at which we incur the law of diminishing returns. We know what an excess of food or alcohol can do, do we not? We must retreat from some of our sexual pursuits to an area within that natural border which represents safety, and re-assess our practices. . . .

The red flag is up!

Tom ended the installment on a lighter note, needling a study that suggested simply visiting the Castro, the heart of the gay ghetto, might be unsafe. "I for one would not avoid the Castro on the basis of that study," he wrote, "unless there was the likelihood of my being raped repeatedly by a small army of unmarried males over the age of 15, and that, in my experience in the Castro, is highly unlikely."

In the final installment Tom's message was rather self-serving, advocating participation in the Gay Games as a possible antidote to the AIDS crisis. But he concluded soberly: "Those of you old enough will remember the 1940s and 50s as a time of great commitment and very little individual freedom. The 60s and 70s with all the new countercultures were about individual freedom and very little commitment. We're now in the 80s and what is beginning to characterize them is again making commitments. . . . Our freedoms will be protected in that way.

"We'd better begin thinking clearly what it really means to be gay."

January 2, 1985

Today was Grandpa's birthday. I gave him a card from you and a framed picture of you and me. He asked me to give you and Mom a kiss when I see you. Gladly. I took Grandpa to the hospital today for his radiation and talked to the doctors. It looks grim, but Grandpa could have a short time to live or a long time and either could be pleasant or full of pain.

If Grandpa's present condition is what can be expected, then I wish for a quick and painless episode. But if he could be free of pain and nausea, then of course I would ask for more heroic measures. I am anxious to see him comfortable whatever the case—and I am anxious to get home and prepare for the events of 1985.

The doctor, it turns out, did his internship at Brookdale Hospital just three years after I did mine there. We had a long talk and knew a lot of people in common. Tomorrow I will go to New York City and take Enge to see his doctor.

Besides cooking and cleaning and shopping, I watch TV with Grandpa—it's an education to see the tripe that passes for entertainment. How I pray you will not be addicted to what network television has to offer—it is truly an opiate. I am now reading the "Family Album of the Romanovs," the last royal family to rule Russia before the revolution in 1917.

I am changing Grandpa's medicine around. I am sure some of the medications are causing his nausea. I asked the hospital to draw extra tests to show or confirm what I think—I'm sure he will feel better in a few days.

The news on television is all about violence, and intolerance, and greed—how can your Mom and I prepare you for all this? We can try to give you balance.

Tom wrote notes to himself, trying to organize and understand his own thoughts: *The death of gay life—the death of those institutions built on the theme of sex*, he mused. *The homosexual community will not disappear—it will evolve. Those who do not change their sex practices will die.*

He came to the conclusion that the institution that in many ways symbolized his own liberation had to go. The baths had to be closed, he wrote. The potential for disaster was simply too great.

Many of the erotic capitalists savaged him, and so did many of their erotic consumers. How could he attack free enterprise, free choice? Wasn't he giving in to the homophobes? Wasn't this what they wanted—to incite fear in the gay community, to cause panic, to alter and punish and destroy the gay lifestyle?

Sara's pregnancy was no small event. In the early 1980s, it was exceedingly uncommon for a gay woman to be carrying a child, and the fact that it was Tom Waddell's child, the son or daughter of one of the more prominent members of the gay community, intensified the interest and the controversy. Sara was bold or foolish, dependent or independent, heroine or villain; the judgments were as varied, and sometimes as unpredictable, as the people who handed them down.

KAISER FOUNDATION HOSPITAL
San Francisco, Calif

BABY	*Lewinstein Jessica*
MOTHER	*Sara*
DATE OF BIRTH	*August 31, 1983*
TIME	*3:55 a.m.*
WEIGHT	*6 lb 5½ oz*
LENGTH	*21"*

I'm a GIRL!

The doctor watched the delivery of his child. "When I saw the umbilical cord," Tom said, "I thought it was a boy."

· · ·

Only a few days later, he made another small mistake. Thinking he was looking in Jessica's baby book, he came across an entry in Sara's diary that left him devastated.

Tom read:

July 15, 1983

Experienced my first Lamaze class with Tom, Chris and Lindy. I'm so in love with Chris and so very much love Lindy to no end. She is wonderful. So supportive and feels so good. Chris is changing and growing, too. I love to watch it—even though it has its moments.

I love Tom, but not the way he wants me to. It was *too hard* at the class. I don't want Tom touching me. I want Chris or Lindy to touch me (massage). It hurt me emotionally much more than I anticipated. I have to talk to Tom. I cried all night and all morning. . . . I want him involved, but not 50/50 and not in that heavy emotional way. I *love* women and he's very much wanting to be a father. I need my legal papers worked on immediately. I don't ever want a problem with my child.

It's *my baby*—and I want to share it with the women I love first—then Tom. I hope this isn't an ideal. This is my reality.

Tom's gut reaction was to withdraw or at least retreat from the relationship, but Sara salved his bruised feelings, assuring him that he could share in the raising and shaping of his daughter.

Soon after Jessica's arrival, Tom received the Harvey Milk award for community service, presented annually at the Cable Car Awards in memory of the former San Francisco supervisor. Milk was the first openly gay elected official in the United States, and he had been shot to death in 1977. Mayor

Feinstein presented the award and thanked Tom for bringing the Gay Games to her city.

The Internal Revenue Service, after eighteen months of indecision, granted the SFAA tax-exempt status, accepting Tom's argument that its purposes were essentially educational and charitable. The USOC, however, was not so kind. In February 1984, a United States District Court judge granted the USOC a permanent injunction, barring the SFAA's use of the word "Olympic."

At least the SFAA had company. The USOC was trying to shoot down "Olympics" everywhere. It forced a Colorado high school to abandon "Olympian" as the name of its yearbook but failed to force a Philadelphia eatery to change its name from the Olympic Restaurant and Pizzeria. "I have more of a right to use the word 'Olympic' than they do," insisted the owner, Jimmy Prinos, who was Greek.

Nationality was not always a sufficient defense. After spending $25,000 in legal fees resisting the USOC, Nick Agathis of Newark, New Jersey, changed his bus company's name from Olympic Trails to the more acceptable Olympia Trails. Even the March of Dimes gave in, renaming a fund-raising campaign originally called the Reading Olympics—pledges to the charity were based on the number of books a child read— rather than fight the USOC in court. The USOC said the March of Dimes could keep the money it had already raised.

The Special Olympics, with the wealth and power of the Kennedy family behind it, was granted a dispensation by the USOC. But disabled athletes who entered the Paralympics wound up in the World Wheelchair Games, and children competing in the Olympics of the Mind found themselves rerouted to the Odyssey of the Mind.

Against the SFAA, however, the USOC was not satisfied with merely an injunction. In mid-1984 the Olympic Committee filed a suit demanding that the SFAA and Dr. Thomas Waddell pay its legal fees. The district court again ruled in the

USOC's favor, found SFAA and Tom Waddell to have been willful and deliberate trademark infringers, and ordered them to pay legal costs of $96,600. The court froze Tom's assets and placed a lien on his Albion Street home.

January 3, 1985

I feel so lonely. I spent the day going back and forth taking care of Enge and Grandpa. New York depressed me. All the grayness and the cold and the survival mentality, all the reasons I left New York in 1970 came back to me today. Enge was so cantankerous I left the house for an hour and walked about Chelsea, where I had spent about ten years going to school and in medical training. It seemed bleaker than ever.

I took Enge to his eye doctor, down in the Village, which is the most interesting part of the city to me—but even that was cold and depressing.

Back to Grandpa about 5:30 and I must make some decisions. I need to get back to San Francisco. I really don't mind taking care of Enge and Grandpa, but I am not taking care of myself—and taking care of you is taking care of myself.

At this moment, I am thinking I must quit the Games, the ACLU and most other activities and begin to enjoy my life again—fully. I want my zeal for living to be infectious to you, and that will not happen in my present bind of commitments.

The relationship between Tom and Zohn never collapsed, but it did waver. Both were set in their ways, accustomed to giving orders and having them carried out. Zohn lived for a few months in the cottage behind Albion, but he and Tom argued much of that time, and Zohn moved back to his own home. Their relationship fared better at a distance.

Tom traveled a great deal in 1984—to Massachusetts in

the spring to introduce Sara and Jessica to Enge and The Farm, to Canada to promote the Games, to Africa with John Hall of the Dunies to feed his wanderlust. Enge was not exactly charming toward Sara and Jessica; he made it clear that he would rather see Tom alone. He was jealous to the point of rudeness, so rude that he almost reduced Sara, who did not cry easily, to tears. When she offered him Jessica to hold, he declined. Sara did, however, impress some of the other regulars at The Farm: She watched Tom and another ex-jock trying to hit a Wiffle ball one day, and she said, "Here, let me show you how to do it," and she grabbed the ball and a bat and swung and connected, and the ball sailed off and shattered a window on the second floor of the barn. "Oh, my God," Sara groaned. "Enge is going to kill me!"

Tom finally was able to view Enge with some objectivity, to temper his love and his gratitude with the knowledge that his mentor, besides being old and ornery, was not only jealous of his other relationships but also jealous of his success. Enge felt, with some justification, that he had created Tom, and he expected Tom to be loyal enough to respond to his whims.

Ironically, as Tom began to recognize and acknowledge Enge's faults, his feelings toward his father began to change, too. He had spent little time with his biological parents in the sixties, and less in the seventies. When he visited with his father in 1981, when his second wife was ill, and again in 1984, when she had died, Tom realized how little his father had gotten out of life materially and emotionally. He felt sorry for him, and the sadness, mixed with guilt, seemed to turn, as if by alchemy, into love.

January 5, 1985

I think this may be a very scary year—and yet I am optimistic that whatever effort it takes to keep my dignity will be well worth the price. It's about the easiest attribute to live with when everything else seems bleak. A little self-esteem is powerful energy.

Last night, when I returned from Manhattan, I had a talk with Grandpa. Told him about the "Dune" movie I went to and how I walked out of it in disgust. It was beginning to ruin my enjoyment of the book.

I then went to two gay bars which catered to "older men," as they say in the vernacular, which means that all the patrons are either men who believe they are "older" or men who like to be with older men. There were all ages, though the young men were far outnumbered.

It was interesting to see and feel New Yorkers—they give off a great energy and it is somewhat intimidating to me and it always leaves me behaving defensively while I'm in New York—something I must deal with—that strange fear of New York and, particularly, New Yorkers!

I met a man from Brazil who was in lust and we had a fun conversation, though he was not remotely part of my fantasy for the evening. I found I liked him, and I could feel close to him, but when he began getting a bit drunk and more aggressive about his intentions for the evening, I decided it was time to head home. I had wanted something special and exciting and, of course, safe to happen, but since I didn't want anything less than that, I preferred to settle for fantasy. Such satisfying little treats we make of our fantasies. I hope you, Jessica, will allow them to enrich your life.

I came back to Grandpa's and I was a bit stoned and tipsy. I heard Grandpa stir and then walked in to see him awake. I sat on the bed and we held hands and talked. We said very loving and tender things to each other, and I wept when I told him how helpless I felt to make his pain less. But he, so dignified, said, "There is nothing more you can do. I love you, Tommy."

Today—a mad race. Off to Nyack to pick up Mary

[Menaker, Danny's mother] and we drove to New York and had an hour together at a Burger King, her first visit, my last. We had a wonderful talk. She's such a loving and caring woman. I like her great strength. She is a person who knows precisely who she is, and I find that most attractive.

Then to Enge and several hours of restlessness and friction. He is very demanding and cantankerous again, and I indulge him to my capacity, which is quite large, but every now and then I lose it and jump into a game of words with hidden meanings, innuendo and veiled accusations.

Just spoke to Mom and told her my situation here. I cannot leave until I'm sure my father will be comfortable. Perhaps I will be here at least another week.

And yet there is so much to do in San Francisco, and most of all—you. Jessica, I miss you so. I want to watch you grow and blossom and I have so many things to talk to you about and show you.

January 9, 1985

It's difficult to tell one day from the other. I've settled into a routine with Grandpa—not unpleasant at all—but beneath the surface of the routine there is such a profound sadness. I love my Dad more all the time—and I feel so helpless.

I try to make him smile as often as possible and I am now so tuned in to him I can anticipate his needs even before he can. I know it makes him feel good when that happens.

Tonight, when I sat on his bed to say goodnight, he stared at me, and I was stunned into silence because I could see the question in his eyes. He was asking, *Why is this happening?* He finally did say, "I never thought anything like this would happen."

I could only say, "There's never any reason, Dad."

Yesterday I went to care for Enge, and mostly I did

chores and sat silently in the living room. I cannot talk to Enge any more. There is no basis for any conversation. He has his thoughts and he does not welcome contradictions, so I listen, often without comment.

I had dinner with an old friend, Sam, a Greenwich Village character who was one of the people who educated me about 25 years ago. Sam is now 72 and we enjoyed our dinner, but I noticed the preoccupation with himself and the extreme self-centeredness. Is this what all of us can look forward to when we're elderly? Are we going to lose the ability to be receptive and interested in the world? Grandpa doesn't strike me as being self-centered; in the midst of his pain, he remains sensitive to everyone else. And Mary, she seems so young for her nearly 80 years. If it is not inevitable that we turn so dramatically inward, then I must study this phenomenon even closer and watch for the pitfalls. I will be 66 (I hope) when you are 20 and I want to be someone you will enjoy being near, not someone you owe a duty.

I will be home in less than a week. I hate leaving Grandpa, but I also must be near you.

January 10, 1985

Same routine for most of the day—but then tonight, while I was brushing my teeth, I noticed some white patches on my tongue. Sweetheart, I hope it's nothing, but there is the possibility that this is an early sign of AIDS. The horror I feel and the fear of leaving you before you ever know me is my greatest concern. I don't know what to do or what to think at this moment, but I do know I must suppress all morbid thoughts until I can get more information.

I tucked Dad into bed as I usually do and asked him about his decision on whether to stay here or go to California to stay with me (where I think he will probably pass away).

He is very frightened about traveling, but he's also frightened about being alone, so he will wait a few weeks and then come out for a visit—a good compromise, I think, though I fear he will be too weak by then.

January 12, 1985

What a nightmare yesterday was. I woke at 4 a.m. to hear my Dad retching in the bathroom. I hadn't slept all that well and was very drowsy, but I could see that he was distressed and in trouble. There were cotton balls of blood all over the sink and floor and tub, and Dad was sitting on the john with his head bent over a big pan to catch the blood from his nose.

We tried everything to stop the bleeding, but nothing would work. Finally, at 5:30, I got him dressed and drove him to the E.R. at Beth Israel. Of course I argued with all the staff about what should be done, but only the more secure individuals would listen. So we had to go through a series of (avoidable) trial-and-error maneuvers before Dad was adequately treated. He was kept for the day and given two units of packed cells to restore the blood he'd lost. I began feeling dizzy and nauseated and then had one of the worst headaches I can ever remember. PLUS, I was running to the bathroom every few minutes to check my tongue to see if the lesions I thought were "thrush" were any better or worse.

My eyes were red and my eyelids were flaky from seborrhea, and I generally felt like my entire body was quitting on me.

I finally managed to get to sleep last night and then up several times to keep Dad company while he tried to clear out his nose again.

So here I sit—having just discovered some gray-white patches in the back of my throat as well. I think I am dying, and my reaction is one of feeling depressed.

To end on an up note, I had a dream about you and Mom last night. The three of us were all in your room and we were playing—you were laughing at something Mom and I were doing—and the sight and sound of you was the most wonderful feeling imaginable.

I felt so totally happy!

January 13, 1985

Yesterday, I went to New York City to spend the day with Enge and say my "goodbye" to him—I always feel it will be my *last* goodbye and it is always difficult.

I still felt the "unknown" presence of possibly having AIDS, so I was not in the best of spirits. In any case, I managed good humor all day and made it very pleasant, bathing Enge and shaving him and rubbing him down with lotion and making him laugh. Our goodbye was poignant and he let me know how much he loved me and acknowledged that he felt loved. He came to the doorway to the hall and waited until I disappeared into the elevator.

I then went to dinner with my friend Sam, who invited someone I wanted to meet—Tim Desmond, who was one of a very few people who spent time with the Shah of Iran after he was deposed. I have a plot for a book about the Shah, and Tim has exactly the kind of inside information I need to make it entirely believable—even authentic.

Today was all for my Dad. We both wept when we talked about my leaving tomorrow. I love him very much and I will miss him. I somehow think this will be the last time we speak to each other face to face.

But tomorrow—I will see you at the airport. I can hardly wait, my darling.

January 17, 1985

Well, the meeting at the airport was anything but auspicious. You seemed to not know me at all and would not even look at me—the same kind of treatment that drives your mother crazy. I just decided to wait for you to recognize me rather than push it.

Zohn got in a terrible snit when you pulled a condom from my coat pocket. He drove us home like a madman, and in total silence.

I'm glad to be home, but it's not going to be easy to stabilize the crazy things going on around me.

You and Mom and I must make our future plans more definite in terms of another child, Mom and me getting married, financial arrangements, responsibilities, etc., etc.

I must resolve my relationship with Zohn. We've both been very unhappy for too long. He wants a marriage between us, and I don't. In this era of AIDS, it's sensible to be monogamous or even celibate, but I still can't bring myself to that kind of commitment to Zohn.

The lawsuit with the USOC looms large and I still don't know where it's going. I'd like to get it resolved so I can stop thinking about it.

You have a cold and you are cutting your first molars— very cranky—and we are all just bending over backwards to make you comfortable. You are an exceptional child, my dear. Lots of personality and expression, and you are interested in everything and amazingly gregarious. We all know you are special—but I don't think we can hide our bias.

I am avoiding a lot of things, but I did acquiesce to a speech at Cal State Hayward, a presentation at the David Awards and a repeat trip to Vancouver for their summer games. I'm sure I'll jump into other things as well, but for now it's a bit of lay back.

January 19, 1985

Last night I left you off at Mom's and decided it would be a movie for me, but no one else wanted to go. I went alone only to find it sold out. So I went window shopping along Castro Street and watched the crowd. There are so many people in the world, and we know so few. And I went to dinner at the "Welcome Home," a pleasant, gay, greasy spoon. Then afterward out in the street there was some excitement. It was the Gay Freedom Day marching band in their uniforms, plus the Sisters of Perpetual Indulgence, and they were passing out pom-poms for a football rally. It was like being back in college. I got into it right away. I was waving my pom-pom with hundreds of others and singing the 49ers' song. The Sisters had the words painted on posters for us to read. The TV cameras were catching all of this for the evening news.

I stayed until my enthusiasm waned and then came home. Zohn had gone out and I decided to sleep the night with Wil [a professor who was then living in the cottage behind Albion]. I crept into his bed and cuddled up. He partially awoke and acknowledged me, cuddled closer and went back to sleep, and I shortly thereafter. It was pleasant and comfortable. Wil and I have loved each other for many years, and while we each disapprove of each other in some small ways, there is still a great deal of love and respect to sustain us. He and I will always be friends, just as Eric and I will.

On Friday night, there was an auction at Amelia's, around the corner from home. Mom was responsible for the preparation that went into the event. She collected prizes, had graphics made up, arranged and directed the entire fair. It netted around $3,600, and it showed everyone what a remarkable woman your mother is. She also won the annual David Award for outstanding sportswoman of the year, which is basically a popularity contest. She's been busy.

I went to a party tonight, after spending a few hours with you. You have been in a lot of pain for several days now, and it is difficult for all of us because we hate to see you suffer. But I also know that it is something that we all must experience, and so I try to make it less important for its pain and more important for its introspection. One should not waste or wallow during periods of pain. These periods serve a valuable purpose; they allow you to put pain in perspective, all kinds of pain in all kinds of perspectives.

But here you are with pain and swelling of your gums and an upper respiratory infection—and you are such a champ about it. You allow yourself to be distracted from the pain—and you will even play. I applaud you, my darling.

I've been teaching you to touch flowers and animals softly and tenderly by whispering "Gentle!" when you touch them, and you always respond. But you are ill, and Zohn came up to watch you while I went first to a reception for Congressman Barney Frank of Massachusetts and then to give a short speech and make a presentation on "unity" at the David Awards. Mom and Chris were there, and we then went to Maud's for a drink together. Here at home, you were out for the count.

January 20, 1985

You and I spent the morning together, then over to Mom's where we had a Super Bowl party—I was the only male. You were cranky. Mom was stressed yet we all managed to have a nice time. And, incidentally, the San Francisco 49ers won over Miami, 38–16, to complete a 17–1 season. Of course the entire city is a madhouse tonight.

January 21, 1985

Spent the day with you at Mom's. You have lost some weight
and you are still having a lot of pain in your gums—poor
baby, you still manage to play and sing in spite of your dis-
comfort. I put the new organizer I bought Mom for Christmas
in her closet today. She came home early, feeling wiped out
and on the verge of a cold. It was nice to have the three of
us together even if there's illness. We have a good support system going.

Mom and I need to talk about marriage and a brother or
sister for you.

Tonight I went to a dinner party and wound up pledging
to do a fundraiser for San Francisco AIDS Hospice. I just
couldn't afford to give any money.

January 27, 1985

Last night, my darling, you and I went to a dinner party. Interesting group of gay men, some writers, some lawyers and
bankers.

You have adopted a blanket for security. Mom has one,
and I have another that feels the same, but has a different design. I don't know if you are aware of the difference, but I
prefer to think you are.

I am in trouble. The USOC has frozen all my personal as-
sets and is trying to take $96,000 from me—I fear they will
succeed. And even more depressing are the arguments I've
been having with the new executive director of the Games.
Had I not made such an investment in the project, I would
let it go.

I am going back into medical practice. Decision made several days ago. I have an office I once practiced in before,

about eight years ago. I am excited, but there is much preparation to be done. Eric will be my receptionist.

Zohn is staying with his friend Larry tonight. Larry may pass away before sunrise—I hope that is so—it will be best for all. I am very proud of Zohn for his dedication and his love. My father waxes and wanes. I am not sure from one day to the next what I wish. If he is in pain, then I wish for a quick death. But I will miss him. We speak every other day.

February 4, 1985

I fear that 1985 is taking a turn for the worse. Somehow, I am not going to let this be a bad year for us, my darling. Mom is worried and depressed about money and commitments. I have loaned her $10,000 and I have to service the loan at 15%. I wish I could give her the money, but I am strapped and in debt myself. I don't spend a lot of time worrying about money—it's always there to be made—but it's tight just now.

I called my Dad early this morning, and he was slipping badly. Tonight I tried again, no answer. I spoke to my brother, who said Dad was doing very poorly. I suddenly felt very sad about my father. It was not so bad when I could talk to him—even though he was in pain, he was still there. Now he's not in much pain, but he isn't really there. For the first time, I feel like weeping. I may have to go to him soon.

I am arranging to open my medical practice on March 1. Takes lots of preparation—refresher courses, malpractice insurance, equipment, forms, procedures.

My father may die soon. At least he will not see me die of AIDS.

February 5, 1985

My dear Jessica, I believe I have just made a conscious decision to die. I am sitting in my study looking at a picture of
you and I am wondering if I have harmed you or Mom in any
way.

I went to a doctor this morning. . . .

February 6, 1985

My darling, I am somewhat overcome with feelings—I'm not
even sure what I'm thinking. I arrived in New Jersey this evening to attend my Dad's funeral. He died yesterday at 6:45
p.m.

I was writing to you yesterday when my brother called to
give me the news. I was about to tell you that I may have
early signs of AIDS and if that is so, there is a good chance
that I will die within the next two years. I am not afraid of
dying, but the disease is so victimizing, my life will not be the
same again.

I got Mom, Zohn, Eric and Roger together and spoke to
all of them at the same time. I wanted them to know just
what the facts were so we could all deal with the necessities
in a reasonable fashion. Everyone understood, but Mom was
particularly upset. It was quite a shock to her, and she stood
off by herself and wept.

Later that afternoon, I got the news about my Dad. I
spent the day extricating myself from my planned medical
practice. It just made no sense to pursue it. Then I prepared
to come here.

And now I am sitting in my Dad's apartment where he
and I had three inseparable weeks together and connected so
well, and he is no longer here. I just went through some of his

belongings and found hundreds of photographs of his entire lifetime—and of course a good part of mine as well.

I am so sad, I must stop now. I am going to sleep (I hope) in his room and think about the man. I miss him so.

Tom had recognized, and his doctor confirmed, that he had several of the early symptoms of AIDS. But he was, at this point, an ARC—someone diagnosed with AIDS-Related Complex, HIV-positive, but not fatally infected with full-blown AIDS, not yet. "I thought, *Okay, I'm an ARC,*" Tom said, "*but I pray that I'm one of those ARCs that doesn't go on to full-blown AIDS.* Well, I lost. I was one of those that went on."

February 14, 1985

I have been going to the hospital for some special tests to rule out pneumocystis pneumonia. Death is very much on my mind these days, and I find my time with you to be so precious. Mom knows what state I am in and she is being so kind about it. We are trying not to think of the possibilities and we are all meeting in Los Angeles at Grandma's home (the three of us), and then Mom and I are going to Las Vegas to get married.

Whoopee! I've wanted that for a long time.

Mom's nervous, and we're both like children about it. Wonder what we'll use for rings. I think I'll write a little poem to her and read it at the ceremony.

Today you shone like the brightest little star. All day—so animated, so alive, so joyful. Mom had her 8th Artemis anniversary. I came late because of an ACLU meeting. But there you were, brought to the party by Eric, Roger and Zohn. You were singing and dancing and entertaining everyone—and everyone knew that we all had somebody special. Some woman came up to me and said that Jessica was so lucky—the world

should be full of children who have fathers like you—I felt
such pride!

But you are you, and my pride is just an internal indulgence. You will be a remarkable *individual* and many people
will love you.

I walked home after dancing and enjoying myself.

On the way, I thought, "What will my friends tell Jessica
about me?"

February 24, 1985

Your mother and I are now your legally married parents. We
eloped to Las Vegas, Nevada, on February 18, and were married in a chapel on "The Strip." We bought rings, hired a limousine and took a suite at the MGM, got all dressed up (me
in blazer and slacks, white shirt and tie, Mom in a tan dress
and a striped gray-and-white wool coat). She looked like a
Polish princess, strong and hearty and bold—these qualities
make your mother a startlingly beautiful woman.

We were married about 4 p.m. after getting our license at
the marriage bureau (300 per day). Then we toasted ourselves
with champagne, took the limo back to the hotel and got
ready to gamble. We both love to gamble, as I'm sure I've already told you. I lost a lot, Mom lost some. We had dinner
and saw a real kitsch show at the Grand and then lost some
more money.

I was feeling very sick. I have a fever and cough and
headache, but I took some medicine to make me feel
better—I didn't want to ruin Mom's good time. And she did
have a good time, though she did expect to win big—and
didn't.

The following night, we both won a lot—early. I pulled in
the bucks on the slots and blackjack and took Mom to dinner
and then lost it all.

So what! I decide before I gamble just how much I will permit myself to lose. If I win, great, but where do you stop? So I always figure the odds are in their favor and I look to have a good time for what I spend.

We got no sleep the second night and I flew back to San Francisco early in the morning. Mom flew to Los Angeles to be with you and to take care of [her sister] Mina, who was about to deliver. She did, today, and you now have a cousin, a little girl who is a year and a half younger than you. Perhaps you will be good friends.

I came back to lecture at Cal State Hayward to a sociology class and talked about the philosophy of the Games. It went well, but I was wiped out.

I came home and took a pill and went to bed. More fever, more cough. I got up on Thursday and flew to San Diego, where I was to speak to several groups of gay men and women and present a picture of the Games and ask for money. I slept all day and attended two evening affairs. They were well organized and well publicized, but poorly attended. I made some real friends for the Games, but couldn't raise much money.

Mom is down in L.A. with you. She will bring you back in the next few days, and I will have you for a while so Mom can get some things done.

You were amazing when I saw you at Grandma's house. All of your Mom's family was there, and you kept us all entertained. You dance so effortlessly, and you are so delicate and charming and bright as a precious stone. You are a miracle to me, my sweet darling, and Mom feels exactly as I do. We are all wed to each other.

I am quite ill, and of course worried about it—and worried about dozens of other things. I'm not certain I'm not simply indulging myself in some unhealthy way—thereby making me sick—and giving me an excuse for failure. I will talk more of this at a later date, but I am concerned that I have created a perilous situation for myself.

February 26, 1985

Tonight, sweetheart, your Mom and I blasted our anger in unison at a meeting of the Executive Committee for the Games. I first made a speech about leaving the Games, and I am now on a leave of absence till I'm ready to go back. I don't know if I ever will go back.

I went to the doctor today, after picking you up. I am still having fever and coughing. I am now to get a consultation on the lesions on my tongue—hairy leukoplakia, it's called—and it may be a precursor to full-blown AIDS.

I'm trying to get into an experimental program. My health situation is one of the major reasons for letting go of the Games. I don't know how much of a role stress plays in the disease, but I want to be around for you and Mom and Zohn and Eric and Roger.

You and I had a wonderful day together. We have taught you to say "Mooo" when we mention a cow. Today you were in the stroller looking up at the sky—and you said "Mooo"—I said, "There's a cow up there"—and when I looked up, there in the middle of the bright blue sky, was the MOON!

You are so wonderful.

Tom did not write again in Jessica's journal for almost two years—not that there was any paucity of news. In the interim, Enge Menaker died at the age of ninety, and Tom graduated from ARC to full-blown AIDS, endured his first bout with pneumocystis, and still managed to win a gold medal in Gay Games II.

. . .

One day in the spring of 1985, Jessica was visiting Tom at Albion and enjoying a ride on the back of Hannah, the giant schnauzer owned by Eric and Roger. Hannah was a week younger than Jessica but considerably larger and seemed to take great pleasure in carrying Jessica about. But when she slipped off Hannah's back, fell to the floor, and began to cry, Tom leaped up, shouted, "She's attacking my daughter," which wasn't true, and lunged at the dog.

Hannah elected to retreat and lumbered toward the doggy door leading to the garden and safety. Furious, Tom decided to kick Hannah. He missed. His swinging foot hit the wall instead and he broke a toe, the bone jutting out through the skin.

Eric took Tom to the emergency room at Kaiser Permanente Medical Center for treatment, and Jessica accompanied them. Tom's foot was x-rayed, and as he and Jessica waited for the results a nurse walked up to Tom and told him what a cute daughter he had. That made his foot feel better.

"You'd better make sure you don't take her up to the fifth floor," the nurse said.

"What's up there?" Tom said.

"That's where they keep the AIDS patients," the nurse said.

"Could she get AIDS just by going up there?" Tom asked.

"It's possible."

Tom shook his head. "That's not the way I understand it," he said. "I believe it takes intimate sexual contact to acquire AIDS."

"Well, you'd better keep her off the fifth floor anyway," the nurse said, "because she might get one of those strange diseases."

She was referring to the "opportunistic" organisms that attack people whose immune systems have been weakened or destroyed by the AIDS virus.

"I don't think that's possible," Tom said. "Those 'strange diseases' that kill AIDS patients aren't that strange. They're caused by organisms that you and I have in our bodies. It's just that our immune systems are healthy enough to fight them off."

"Well, I can see there's just no talking to you," the nurse said.

Tom was incensed. He felt the nurse was gratuitously spreading false and inflammatory information about people with AIDS. He complained to the hospital, and within two weeks the nurse was suspended, pending an investigation.

He told the story to Bill Mandel, who faithfully reported the details in his column in the *Examiner*. The column was accurate, except for Mandel's description of the injury that led to the incident: "Waddell fell and broke a foot while repairing his Mission District home. . . ."

Tom never mentioned to Mandel that he had broken his toe trying to kick a dog. He realized he would have gotten less sympathy.

Two days before Christmas 1985, Enge Menaker died, fulfilling the second of Tom's sad predictions for the year. (Elmer Flubacher's death was the first.) Tom himself had survived, but he knew that, barring a miracle, the virus raging in his body would not allow him to live through many more holiday seasons.

In January 1986, Tom visited The Farm for the final time to attend a memorial service for Enge.

Then he went back to San Francisco to brace himself for Gay Games II and the full onset of his disease.

•   •   •

In the spring of 1986, Tom worked feverishly, often literally—he could not shake a low-grade fever that wavered between 99 and 100 degrees—preparing for Gay Games II. But where once the Games were Tom's dream, they had now become, he said, "a nightmare." He felt inadequate, unable to cope with responsibilities he had once handled with ease. He was tired and depressed and angry, alienated even from friends such as Mary Dunlap, the lawyer who was representing him in the continuing battle with the USOC.

He was, not surprisingly, preoccupied with his health. "Of course I have constant thoughts about AIDS," he said. "Nothing new. Trouble is, I don't know how much worrying contributes to the reality of the disease. Which comes first? What causes what?"

A couple of months before the Games, Tom decided he had to escape from everyone, to be alone to "clear my head and make decisions on what is important in my life for as long as I have left."

He drove from San Francisco to Nevada and kept a record of his thoughts: "I am so unhappy these days, confused, mixing everything up and consequently being indecisive and irritable. All my friends, what is left of them, are concerned, and so am I."

He stopped at Donner Lake to look at vacation homes and paused in Reno to gamble and to stare at the tourists, "mostly elderly couples, retired, wearing polyester clothes and spending their social security checks." He found himself "too tired to think—about anything except Jessica. I love her so and I miss her. My health feels so tenuous and I fret about how long I've got to be with her. I want to leave her something she will love and enjoy. She is such a water freak and I want to find her a place to call her own where she can escape and play. A vacation home on a lake."

In Tahoe City one night, Tom checked into the only motel with a vacancy, a "Fantasy Inn" catering to the "adult" crowd. His room offered a circular water bed covered with red ersatz velvet and surrounded by mirrors at every conceivable angle. "I watched an 'adult' movie," Tom reported, "and decided that the porno filmmakers were all sick. The plots are non-existent, the acting also non-existent and the depictions of hetero-sex are no more attractive or exotic than watching dogs fornicate. I can easily say that my heterosexual experiences were far more exciting than those flicks."

His thoughts prompted Tom to make a list of what he considered to be his heterosexual experiences, "my straight affairs," a short list starting with Quenby Sameth and ending, six women later, with Sara Lewinstein, who probably never aspired to appear on such a roll. "Interesting," Tom mused. "The women in my life tend to be Jewish, aggressive, pretty and *attractive*, which covers qualities other than physical beauty. They also tend to be on the plump side rather than the thin." Two of the women, Tom had not forgotten, "had remarkably sexy bodies."

He said he "admired all of them, and they me, and I still do, with the possible exception of Sara, whom I love dearly. I'm just not certain of the depth of feeling she has toward me. Some of the time I feel she just sees me as a good contract; other times, I feel genuine concern. It's mostly the former, but it's OK. I think she's an incredible woman and mother."

Early in July, troubled by nausea, headaches, fatigue and a persistent cough, he submitted to a series of tests. "Tom, I'm sorry to tell you this," said his physician, Dr. William Strull, "but the biopsy was positive for pneumocystis."

Tom wrote in his journal: "So there it is, the news which every gay man fears."

He was no longer an ARC. He had AIDS. It was, he knew, a death sentence.

He was aware that he might live a few months or even a year or two, but no longer. He could look forward to increased pain and, worse, growing disorientation and a variety of ailments that would sap his strength and his will. And yet, strangely, once he knew for certain that he was approaching death, his mood seemed to lift; his unhappiness diminished, and his preoccupation with death was supplanted by a preoccupation with life.

When he learned that Tom had AIDS, Zohn Artman decided to move for the first time into the main house at Albion. "I wanted to be there to be of help to him, you know," Zohn explained. "I mean—this is my guy."

Zohn recognized that their relationship was not an easy one. "He's a leader, and I'm a leader," Zohn said. "And he was always trying to tell me what to do, and I was always trying to tell him what to do, and we clashed."

But despite the clashes and the strains, Zohn felt that the bond between them endured. "I've never had an adult peer friendship in the way I have with Tom," he said. "I can't speak for him, but I know we are still very bonded."

Ten days after Zohn moved into Albion, he himself was diagnosed with AIDS. "And I go to the hospital for a month," he said, "and I know it was upsetting to Tom that when I got out of the hospital I didn't come back to Albion. I had the strongest gut-level feeling that I did not want to live or put Tom through living in an AIDS ward. You're groaning and moaning and you're up during the night, and you have different medicinal schedules and needs, and I just didn't see it working for either one of us in the long stretch. I didn't want to put the stress of anguishing over each other under the same roof on us."

. . .

When Zohn learned that he, too, had AIDS, he traveled East
to say goodbye to his mother, who had never quite come to
terms with his gayness. Zohn was greeted at the airport by a
niece, who told him she had good news for him and bad. He
asked for the good news first, and his niece handed him a
small envelope of cocaine. "The bad news," the young woman said, "is that your mother is telling everyone you have
cancer."

Tom was hospitalized with pneumocystis only two weeks before the start of Gay Games II. But, against his doctor's advice, he checked himself out of the hospital when the Games
began. "If I had to crawl," Tom said, "I was going to be
there."

He formally opened the Games with what he considered
to be the best speech of his life.

> There are approximately four hundred million gay peo-
> ple in this world, around whom a young but vital cul-
> ture has developed. We have our own unique institutions
> and patterns of behavior and to a large extent our own
> language.
>
> It is quite possible that someday the distinctions be-
> tween gay and nongay cultures will become irrelevant,
> but for the nonce, with these Games and the Procession
> of the Arts, we hereby serve notice that we are fully
> vested citizens of the world, with a thriving and bona fide
> culture, and that we are worthy of the respect and es-
> teem of all other citizens of this world.
>
> Today, and this week, we see ourselves as we really
> are—active, productive, creative, and healthy. I hope we
> all experience the sense of self-worth and self-esteem

that is the natural consequence of the activities in this community.

Let the Games begin!

Two days after leaving the hospital, Tom competed in the javelin throw. "I didn't want anyone to give me a medal," he said. "I wanted my own medal." He got his medal, a gold one—and he also got tuberculosis.

In 1982, if it had not been for the suit filed by the U.S. Olympic Committee, Gay Games I might have been totally ignored by the media. But in 1986 the event drew attention not because of an ill-conceived and homophobic legal maneuver but because of an even more unwanted situation, the burgeoning AIDS crisis. In 1982, AIDS was primarily the concern of the gay community; by 1986, the epidemic was global and terrifying. In the U.S., fewer than 1,000 cases of AIDS had been reported to the Centers for Disease Control in 1982. By mid-1986 more than 23,000 had been recorded, and among them was Rock Hudson, the actor whose death in 1985 had shocked and shaken the world.

Gay Games II attracted more than 3,500 athletes from seventeen nations, more than twice as many competitors as in Gay Games I. The second edition brought in $705,000, a profit of $25,000 over the expenditures of $680,000. The Games were flourishing. Their creator was not.

Tom was fortunate enough to get into an experimental program, at Kaiser Permanente, which, ironically, was where he had met the nurse who was so insensitive to AIDS patients. Through the program he received a new medication called AZT free of charge; outside the program, the drug cost as much as $800 a month.

At first Tom found AZT promising; it reduced his symptoms, and restored his energy. But it had to be taken every four hours, and he relied on an alarm clock that rang six times a day to remind him of his medication and his disease. He shrugged off the inconvenience. "It bothers me more when I have to wake up to go to the john," he said.

Tom was fortunate, too, to have an unusually gifted and caring physician in Bill Strull, a Kentuckian who had based himself in California after graduating from Harvard Medical School in 1978. At one time Strull had considered specializing in oncology, but had decided against it because he wanted to cure people, rather than having to deal with death on a constant basis.

And then he happened upon AIDS. In 1981, during his residency, he helped treat one of the first unexplained cases of pneumocystis. "He was a very articulate, very intelligent young man," Dr. Strull recalled, "and none of us could understand why he had pneumocystis. Before then, everyone with pneumocystis pneumonia had it because of some known medical condition for which they had been treated with immune-suppressing drugs, like steroids or something similar. But this patient had none of those risk factors. He died, and we were completely mystified. Just about that time, three or four similar cases were reported in Los Angeles. Three or four cases of unexplained pneumocystis constituted an epidemic. We knew right then we had a problem, but we couldn't fathom how great a problem it would become."

From 1982 through 1984, Dr. Strull was a fellow in health policy and epidemiology. He then returned to clinical practice and soon found that because of his background, AIDS patients were being referred to him.

"I didn't know what I was getting myself into," Dr. Strull said. "It just started happening. I was initially fascinated by the variety of challenges on the medical level, but as I got more and more into it, I realized I was in a very frustrating and, in a sense, no-win situation. My patients clearly were not going to live forever.

"I couldn't ask for a more gratifying population of patients—men similar to myself in educational background, in interests, in age, in so many ways—people easy to get friendly with, people you begin to cherish as friends as well as patients. And yet I knew I was going to lose every one of them. Not most of them. All of them. The burgeoning number of these patients and the increasing severity and diversity of their problems were, at times, frankly overwhelming."

Bill Strull was not himself a member of the gay community, but his life was intertwined with it. For a while, his social schedule seemed to consist almost entirely of attending memorial services.

Tom was a typical patient, in the sense that he and Strull were able to share numerous intense, prolonged conversations, that they got to know each other well, that Strull would become preoccupied with Tom's illness each time he had to be hospitalized. But Tom was atypical, too, because he was himself a physician, a knowledgeable and insightful physician. "He realized it was difficult for me to take care of him," Strull said. "He encouraged me at times by saying things like, 'I know this is hard on you and I want you to know I appreciate what you're doing, and I know that we're not going to win but that we're going to be together throughout this.'

"The kind of courage Tom showed is, actually, widespread among AIDS patients, more widespread than among my other patients. Many of them will frequently ask me how I'm doing. At times I'm shocked by that, by their concern for me, but I realize they regard me as a friend.

"Tom was lucky enough to be in a very supportive setting among his friends, lovers, wife, and daughter. He had quite a network."

•　　•　　•

When Tom was hospitalized with tuberculosis in August 1986, one of Bill Strull's toughest duties was to tell him that because the TB was contagious, he couldn't attend Jessica's third birthday party. "It was so hard to tell him," Strull remembered. "I thought it would be his daughter's last birthday with him."

It was.

In the fall Tom went public with his sickness. Robert Scheer broke the news in a front-page story in the Los Angeles *Times*:

> SAN FRANCISCO—Dr. Tom Waddell, a tall, muscular blond Greek-god type when he represented his country in the 1968 Mexico City Olympics, still looks pretty good. Lankier now and bearded, in his favorite dress of sweats and sneakers, he still suggests the supple strengths of the man who was once the world's sixth best decathlon competitor. Not bad for a guy pushing 50. Not bad for someone dying of AIDS.

The New York *Times* picked up the article, and I was one of the millions who read it and was moved, who saw in Tom Waddell's life and impending death a story of major significance. I had been covering sports on and off for more than thirty years, always looking for stories that transcended the games, that could provoke laughter or tears, surprise or anger, honest and strong emotions. The variety of Tom's athletic skills, the depth of his determination, coupled with the tragedy of his illness, seemed to bring together everything I had been looking for. I proposed the story to ABC's *20/20*, and not long before Christmas 1986, I traveled to San Francisco to meet Tom Waddell.

December 9, 1986

Dear sweetheart, I am in the process of being interviewed, and it is quite interesting. It's a program called *20/20* and it generally is a treatment of what my life has been about.

The Gay Games have come and gone; they were enormously successful, but about two weeks before the opening ceremonies, I developed a full-blown case of AIDS. It seems like a terrible tragedy, but it's all being handled. There is a lot to explain to you, and I will attempt to do so as my strength permits.

Mom is, of course, confused and upset, and everyone is trying to handle the news as well as possible. It doesn't seem real, but it is.

My greatest concern is for your safety and Mom's safety. Mom had herself tested and, thank God, she was negative, which means that you are negative as well. What a relief.

I was able to pull myself together after my hospitalization and joined everyone for the opening ceremonies, of which there is more than adequate documentation. You will probably get tired of seeing all the things that we have saved for you from the Games.

I have just left the hospital following my second bout of pneumocystis, and it was pretty horrible. I truly did not know if I was going to survive this episode.

My greatest fear is not being around to watch you grow into a woman. I have such hopes for you, and yet they are not hopes I wish to press on you. If nothing else, I hope I can help you understand that you have your own choices, and that we, Mom and I, are available to support what you choose to do.

For three days, as the camera rolled, Tom and I talked about his life and his approaching death, about his loves and his fears. He did not try to fool himself or to fool me. Once, as he was carrying wood to the fireplace, puffing as he came up the stairs, he paused, turned to the camera and said, "Phew! Boy! Anybody wants to lose weight and stop smoking, they ought to get AIDS."

When he took his every-four-hours dose of AZT, he held up his arms, flexed his muscles like a bodybuilder, and said, "Ah, I feel like a new man! I'm alive again."

His good humor and his courage were infectious. The producer and I were as relaxed with him as he was with us.

December 19, 1986

Getting close to Christmas/Hannukah. Everyone is sick. I have seen too little of you over the past two months because of my second bout of pneumocystis, during which I almost died. You have been confused and angry with me because I have not been that "big guy," who is so much fun.

I am trying to recover from the pneumocystis, but there has been one complication after another. I have tuberculosis and I am covered with shingles. You have a cold, and Mom had a cyst removed from her head a few days ago.

I miss you terribly. I don't feel I have much to live for—my body is a wreck, my energy is low and the world is in such a mess—but the one thing that sustains me is the thought of you. You are such a delight. So bright and so beautiful, and you seem to have a great sensitivity. I pray (I don't really pray; I'm not religious) that your outstanding qualities are sensitivity and compassion and intelligence. Good looks are secondary.

December 25, 1986

Strange Christmas. All the adults had a moratorium on gifts, so that we did not go crazy buying things for each other. It was to be *your* day. Mama gave you a Teddy Ruxpin doll ($80 for something you'll use for one week). I got you clothes and some puzzles.

You were not very nice today and in fact you have not been nice to me for several weeks now. I had thought you were angry over my illness and feeling hurt by my neglect, but now I don't think that's the reason. I think Mama is spoiling you and making you thoroughly dependent on her; she is treating you as *her* child rather than *ours*. I feel very peripheral to our "family" lately.

I am getting better from my recent pneumocystis. Am taking AZT, which is an experimental drug, and I have lots of hope for it. There is nothing else, and if it fails to work, then I will probably die within a year.

I have tuberculosis and a terrible herpes zoster infection, and I am weak to the point of being unable to hold you in my arms for more than a few moments. You were cute and funny most of today, but as I said, there are signs of you being spoiled. I doubt it is serious, but it is not fun to be around. And your refusal to hug me or kiss me goodbye sometimes hurts.

January 1, 1987

New Year's Day—gloomy and wet. I had a terrible night with fierce shaking chills and fever of 102 degrees, and I immediately thought of pneumocystis and I quietly began to weep because I have decided I will not go back to the hospital for pneumocystis treatment. It is too painful, and each time it weakens me more. I would have to come off the AZT I am taking, and the chances of not surviving a third attack are quite strong. I don't want to spend a long time suffering and watching everyone around me suffer.

I went to the hospital and the assessment was a bit encouraging. It may not be pneumocystis. It may be my tuberculosis flaring up, which of course has its own attendant problems, but at least it's manageable. Tomorrow I will go for some tests and then get a transfusion.

I shall hang in for as long as it seems reasonable to me.

January 6, 1987

Going to pick you up at school today. Haven't done that in months. I love entering the playground and finding you engaged with the other kids. I love just sitting there and watching you until you discover me or until another child says, "Your daddy's here."

January 10, 1987

You and I had 24 hours together after seeing "Lady and the Tramp" with Mama. It was fun, and so were you.

You couldn't sleep last night because of the street noises, and so we slept together. How beautiful you are. I look at you when you are asleep. I am concerned that you do not spend more time with my friends. You are with Mama and her circle, which is a wonderful group of gay women, but my side is vastly different and I hope you get to know my friends. There are many remarkable characters who would enrich your life.

February 1, 1987

We had a party last night, which was filmed by a TV program called *20/20*, which is doing a 15-minute segment on
your daddy. It is important to me because I think it will
change some people's minds about a number of things. Mom
and I have had some controversy over her participation, but
nothing serious. Mama is being very protective of you (and
herself) and I have no argument with that. She did, however,
acquiesce to an interview and said some very nice things. It
was filmed at one of the lakes in Golden Gate Park.

You are such a delight. I feel such a kinship with you
these days. Somehow I think you know that I am seriously ill
and you are my best friend.

It's difficult being a disciplinarian with you. I find you so
charming and delightful to be with, even when you are being
naughty.

You stayed up at the party last night almost till midnight, just knocking everyone's socks off with your antics and
your humor and your beauty. You are a knockout, sweetheart, and I hope it doesn't ever work against you. Mama and
I put you to bed at midnight—Eric, too, joined in. I read you
some stories and you were soon off to dreamland. You woke
up this morning about 8 a.m. and came to my bed with more
books and asked me to read. I was delighted, but eventually
I left you to go fix your breakfast—in bed, of course. You
watch Sesame Street every Sunday and I often watch it with
you.

We then went to the nearby high school, where the *20/20*
film crew took movies of you and me walking around and
playing together. I can tell you love being outdoors. Perhaps
you need more of that.

As news of Tom's illness spread, he was inundated with
"cures" from friends and strangers—some bizarre, some logi-

cal, all ineffective. He was offered, among other things, experimental doses of lentinan, neurotropin, grycyrrhizin, isoprinocine, organic geranium, and interferon, all of which were available in Japan, as well as the special compounds of home chemists and assorted quacks. Tom declined them all. He stayed with AZT, supplemented by blood transfusions that temporarily lifted his blood count—lowered by AZT—and gave him short bursts of strength and energy.

In February 1987 Tom Waddell and Bill Toomey were reunited, the two Olympians, once close friends, who had drifted apart. I called Toomey, who was then living in southern California, and asked if he would come up to San Francisco to see Tom. He said he would like to very much.

I met Toomey at the San Francisco Airport. He was jowly, clearly overweight, and even though it was morning, the smell of whisky was heavy on his breath. He had fortified himself for the reunion.

I drove him to a practice field where Tom was coaching a group of gay track-and-field athletes. Toomey walked across the field toward Tom, and when they met, they embraced.

"You're looking good," Toomey said.

"I want to feel a lot better than I do," Tom said.

"You're going to make it," Toomey said. "I know that."

Tom shook his head. "Well, I don't know what that means anymore," he said.

"You'll take five, you'll take five years, won't you?" Toomey said.

"I'll take five months."

Toomey stopped, as if struck on the jaw by a jab. "Really?" he said.

"Oh, absolutely," Tom said. He looked at Toomey and added, "My head is in good shape over this." Tom smiled. "I need a new body, but my head's fine."

"Maybe I better talk to you about that," Toomey said, "because mine's not as good as yours."

"I'm not worried about death or dying at all," said Tom Waddell.

Jessica was at the practice field, and Toomey looked at her and said to Tom, "She keeps you going, huh?"

"Oh, God," said Tom, the atheist.

"Is that your energy?" Toomey said.

"She's my energy. She's my little miracle. Sometimes I just go into her room at night and just stare at her. I just find her so beautiful."

"You can't believe you did it, huh?" Toomey said.

When I asked Bill what his reaction was when he first heard Tom was gay, he said he was confused. "But then," he said, "I said, 'Hey, wait a minute, this is my pal, you know. He's never done anything to hurt anybody. He's always helped people. And if this is what his lifestyle is, I accept it.' "

"Then," I said, "when you heard that Tom had AIDS?"

"Oh, I was devastated," Toomey said. "I really was. I tried to call him on the phone. I couldn't even talk, because I was choked up so much. He's a very valuable person to this planet. And I'll always think that."

Toomey admitted that he had once laughed at, and even told, gay jokes, AIDS jokes. "We all say things we don't mean," he said. "We mean things we don't say. When a very close personal friend is afflicted, you begin to realize the depth of this whole thing, and you think, *Holy smokes, this is not a joke anymore.*"

·   ·   ·

One of the things that Toomey admired most about Tom was that he wasn't "just an athlete."

"You see," Toomey said, "when I competed, I didn't want to be known as an athlete. I felt I was a Stanford student, you know. But you get stereotyped as a jock."

"What did you think when you saw Tom today?" I asked.

"Well, I was very apprehensive," Toomey said. "I thought I'd really be tearful and, you know, overly sentimental. And then I realized how under control he is. I mean, here is a human being who is facing not immortality but extinction, which is a terrible word, and he is so at peace with himself, you know, it's scary."

The reunion had a profound impact on Bill Toomey. He stopped drinking that day, and went on a strict diet. Within six months he had shed thirty pounds, and he looked, and acted, like an Olympic champion again.

The days I spent with Tom Waddell had a profound effect on me as well. He was my guide to the gay community of San Francisco, which I approached with preconceptions that swiftly took a beating. He brought me to the Harvey Milk Gay & Lesbian Democratic Club dinner, and the first man I saw when I entered the ballroom grabbed my arm and said, "When the fuck are we going to get a hockey team out here?" Another demanded to know why the San Francisco Giants had made the Kevin Mitchell trade. And I met a gay man who had once been the ultimate macho figure, the Marlboro man in the cigarette ads.

When Mayor Dianne Feinstein bestowed the Harvey Milk Community Service award on Tom, she told him, "I think so highly of you and all you have accomplished. It has been a privilege for me to know and work with you. The entire city, and certainly its mayor, can view all of your accomplishments with great pride, but most particularly your organizing and establishing the Gay Games as a valued new San Francisco tradition."

Tom also received a Cable Car Award from the gay and lesbian community for his work on the Games. "Dear Tom," a letter to him began, "it was so good to see you at the Cable Car Awards last Saturday night. Your courage and your strength inspire me. I think of you often as I struggle to push our state into taking charge of our health policies for our people in need. Thank you for being who you are. Your buddy, Art."

The letter was from Art Agnos, then a state assemblyman and later Dianne Feinstein's successor as mayor of San Francisco.

The Supreme Court of the United States met in March 1987 to consider the case of *San Francisco Arts & Athletics Inc. and Thomas F. Waddell, M.D., v. United States Olympic Committee and International Olympic Committee.*

On the morning of the hearing there was a front-page story in the Oakland *Tribune*, and in the caption beneath a photo of Tom, he stated, "In the court of public opinion, we have already won."

In the photo, though, he himself was clearly losing. Seated on the steps of Albion, he looked gaunt and pale, his eyes sunken, his hair thin, his head resting heavily in his hand. In the article Tom admitted that he had no feeling below his knees. "I have begun to stumble occasionally," he said, "so I really have to watch myself."

Tom was also suffering from toxoplasmosis, a disease that

affects the brain and often strikes people with AIDS. His mental abilities were beginning to deteriorate. In an article in the San Francisco *Examiner*, he struggled to remember the names of cities he feared he would never be able to visit with Jessica. "Isn't this terrible?" he said. "The more I try to remember words, the more they get away from me. Florence, that's it."

Still, he remained upbeat. "I've done so much living," he said. "I feel so fortunate. I've had a terrific time. I'd just like people to know what an adventure life can be."

Tom also remained confident in his fight against the USOC. "We are going to win," he said.

He planned to wear his 1968 Olympic pin in front of the Supreme Court.

March 23, 1987

The Supreme Court case is tomorrow, and a dozen of us have come to D.C. to be at the hearing. It is a major event for me, for the Games organization and for the global gay community.

I have been getting an inordinate amount of press and media coverage over the past several weeks—television, radio, newspapers, etc.—and I feel like a celebrity. There was even an article and pictures in the local gay press when I arrived.

Mom was going to join me, but decided to stay home with you. You both brought me to the airport. How I miss you!

I'm staying with my old and dear friend Suellen in her new house in a black section of D.C. She's wonderful, and we're very close. She has a friend Mike, who has two children, and she's quite happy with her adopted family.

Suellen and I spent the day touring Washington and the museums—the Matisse and the Suleman exhibit at the new Mellon Gallery.

I was stopped on the street by Richard Thomas, a famous actor whom I got to know a few years ago. He's doing a one-man show at the National Theater. A very nice man.

Dinner last night in Maryland in a place I used to eat at frequently 20 years ago when I lived here in D.C.

Tonight, Suellen, Mike, Rikki Streicher [a member of the Gay Games Board], Mary Dunlap [the attorney for the Games] and I had an Indian dinner with curries and sauces—lovely evening.

Tomorrow, the court case!

Mary Dunlap raised five questions before the Supreme Court:

1. In enacting the Amateur Sports Act of 1978 . . . did Congress intend to bestow upon the United States Olympic Committee . . . an exclusive authority to prohibit and enjoin virtually any and every use of the word "Olympic"?

2. Are the well-established tenets of trademark law that generic terms cannot be trademarks and that a party may use an otherwise incontestable trademark fairly to describe its goods or services rooted in First Amendment considerations of preserving freedom of speech and protecting the richness of the human vocabulary against claims of private ownership?

3. Given that USOC was created and chartered by Congress to perform a public function, and given that USOC receives and uses substantial public resources to that end, is USOC engaged in "state action" such that it may not violate the First and Fourteenth Amendments by selecting among diverse potential users of the word "Olympic," based upon speech-suppressing and invidiously discriminatory motives?

4. Can an injunction prohibiting use of "Olympic" by a nonprofit corporation that is tangentially engaged in raising money for its cause be reconciled with trademark infringement and commercial speech precedents that require balancing of the governmental interests in regulating fraudulent commercial speech against free speech interests?

5. If the Amateur Sports Act of 1978 settled nothing more
or less than an incontestable trademark upon USOC as to the
word "Olympic," should that trademark be enforced according
to the standard of proof and defenses to trademark infringement, as well as the standard for awarding attorneys' fees, developed over forty years of litigation under the Trademark Act
of 1946?

March 24, 1987

An historic day—our day in the Supreme Court. It was scary
to see all that legal power concentrated in one room. I did not
get a good feeling about the hearing, but most everyone else
disagrees with me. Mary Dunlap was brilliant in defending
us, and afterward she and I walked out into an enormous col-
lection of TV cameras, microphones and reporters. We conducted interviews for the better part of an hour, and then I
had had enough. I bid my goodbye to Suellen, who was in
tears, and went to the airport where I sit now, waiting to fly
to Detroit and then San Francisco. I probably won't see you
tonight. Mom told me yesterday that you had a high fever
and she kept you home from school.

I brought you a few little gifts. I'll spring them on you
tomorrow.

The saga and the drama in my life continue, in directions
that I sometimes have no control over. I don't know where it's
all going, but one thing is clear: You, my darling, will probably have to contend with some of the consequences. But, fear
not, it will all be interesting.

In the spring of 1987, on a flight from San Francisco, I happened to sit next to the man who was then the Commissioner
of Baseball, Peter V. Ueberroth, whom I had gotten to know
when he organized and ran the 1984 Olympic Games in Los

Angeles. We talked about Tom Waddell and his struggles with AIDS and the USOC, and I told Ueberroth that the Olympic Committee was trying to take Tom's home to satisfy its legal costs. I also said that Tom's dream was to leave the house on Albion Street to his daughter.

Ueberroth reacted sympathetically and promised to look into the matter. It was no empty promise. He got in touch with Robert Helmick, the president of the USOC, and urged Helmick not to pursue financial action against Tom. Helmick responded promptly. "We are taking no action against Dr. Waddell or any of his property," he assured Ueberroth. "Originally, a lien had been filed on his home; however, it was released, and I have directed our attorneys not to reinstitute action even if authorized by the Supreme Court decision. . . . We do not need to harass Dr. Waddell."

"I thought you would like to see a copy of the attached letter from the president of the USOC," Ueberroth wrote to me. "I guess we were successful and you should feel very good for your initiative which brought about this result."

Eventually, but not immediately, the lien on Albion was lifted. I'd like to take the credit, but I'm fairly certain the legal pressure applied by Mary Dunlap and by Judy Baer had much more to do with it.

April 17, 1987

Tax time, Passover and Easter.

I am tucked away in a small charming house in Gualala, a sleepy little town on the Mendocino Coast. You and Mom are with her parents in L.A. and visiting your cousins. What a gang you must be together.

I have not been feeling well. I just stopped my TB medicine because my liver was getting sick. My legs are beginning to give out. I am short of breath and tired all the time and I have no appetite and am losing weight. That's all.

When I am not with you and Mom, I am by myself and sleep a lot.

The segment about me was supposed to be on *20/20* yesterday, but it was postponed, by some powerful executive at ABC, I suppose. I suspect they are responding to pressure from the USOC; that's the way the world works.

So Zohn and I decided to get away for a few days, and here we are, quiet, listening to the sea and occasionally spotting a whale and her calf making their way north to Alaska.

I went with Judy to hear Beethoven's 9th at the symphony two nights ago. I can hardly wait till you are old enough to join me.

You are growing so fast and you are so bright and amusing. Chris and I are sharing the expense of your third year of school, then soon we must try to get you into a good kindergarten. I am not happy with the Montessori school you are attending, but next year perhaps you'll be in Presidio Hill School.

I miss you, even after a single day. You are such a spark and joy in my life, and it is such a challenge to harness and direct all that marvelous energy you possess. I love you.

April 18, 1987

It's been cold, windy, but clear all day. Zohn and I moved to the Old Milano Inn, a Victorian bed and breakfast, very expensive ($108/night) but pleasant and with a spectacular view of a rocky cove. I am not feeling well—very tired, and all sorts of eruptions on my neck and scalp (most of them not visible). My legs are very bad, and I fear I may be crippled soon.

Still, I daydream about moving up here—a place to be away from what seems to me to be an ever more dangerous and unattractive world. I love the serenity and the tranquillity up here. But the only drawback is you. You would probably love it here, but Mama would never tolerate being here. If my health continues to deteriorate, I may consider coming up on my own.

I want to do more writing and sketching and just be more creative without worrying about tenants and repairs and money. We'll see.

11:45 p.m.

Woke up a few minutes before my scheduled pill at midnight. Zohn awoke, too, and now I'm wide awake listening to the waves pound the rocks below. I look out the window and see some beautiful trees illuminated by the house lights on the first floor. And I wonder if anything I do or think has any importance, and even more I wonder if anything has any relevance.

These waves have been pounding these rocks for a few hundred thousand years. I cannot imagine the significance of my being here at this time.

April 19, 1987

Zohn and I have had a very quiet three days together. We have been in three different inns, trying to eat, being quiet, resting when we want and reading a great deal. We take one AZT every four hours around the clock and we stumble from one place to another. We get lots of glances because we are a strange-looking duo. We're both a bit emaciated, with hollow eyes and unkempt hair and beards.

I was reflecting at dinner tonight about all my symptoms and ailments these days, but I also added that in some way these are the dues I am paying for a remarkable lifetime. I have been very fortunate and healthy all my life and I have done everything I ever wanted to do and in an unobstructed fashion. I am pleased to tell you that I have always acknowledged my good health and fortune. I consciously would thank whomever it might have been (sounds religious—it isn't) for all the gifts I've been given. Even when I was competing in athletics, I knew that I was causing some injuries that would plague me when I got older. Well, they are upon me, but they are also a kind of reminder of what I am paying for, and that makes it all quite tolerable.

I feel the same way about AIDS. I would not trade any part of my life to make it different now (silly notion, since it's not even a possibility). I am here and life is still an adventure. I will probably die in the next few years, but it's time to live until then.

I'll see you tomorrow when I pick you up at school. I think of you all the time.

Tom was wrong about pressure from the USOC having forced ABC to postpone the showing of the *20/20* segment about him. The reasons were considerably less Machiavellian, more logistical than political. Two weeks after the original screening date, on April 30, 1987, the segment entitled "To an Athlete Dying Young" aired on *20/20*.

Hugh Downs introduced the piece. "Sometimes when a story's in the news week after week," Downs said, "we begin to get numb—we shut our eyes and close our ears. We know that stories about AIDS patients get that reaction from some people. Maybe it's because so far, there hasn't been one with a happy ending. We wish we could offer that tonight. What we have instead is a story filled with peace and courage. A superb athlete, a remarkable man, has learned to live with his disease, and that is his latest victory in a life of accomplishment."

The story began with Tom and Jessica and Gene Waddell walking and playing in Golden Gate Park: "Sunday in the park. Three generations: a child, her father, and her grandfather. Sunday in the park, sharing precious moments by the bay in San Francisco. Sunday in the park, nothing to disturb the beauty, except . . . the father has AIDS."

Tom spoke first. "If I have any real sadness," he said, "it's over the fact that I probably won't see her in her teens. I mean, if I could hang on that long . . ."

"Oh, you will," Gene said.

"Well, I'm very realistic about it," Tom said. "I—you know, and I don't kid myself."

Later in the segment, Tom stood in the kitchen of his home, talking to his friend John Hall. "You've brought me food when I've asked you to," he said to Hall. "You've cleaned my house, you've done my dishes, you've given me lots of moral support."

"Well, I love you," John Hall said.

"I know you do," Tom said. "That's why I ask you to do those things, because there are times when I get down, and there's John—you know, there's John to provide me with the kind of support that I need."

Zohn Artman, too, appeared in the story and offered his support. "I want to be here when he dies," Zohn said, "because I want to, you know. I'm good at holding hands. I've had six or seven of my friends die in my arms."

At the end of the story, Tom and I were leafing through photo albums and I said, "All of your friends, they're going to miss you so much."

"Our memories serve us well," Tom said, "but, yeah, they will. But I have friends who died that I miss terribly, but—but I get a great joy out of thinking about them."

"And someday," I suggested, "Jessica will look at these pictures and she'll wonder . . ."

Tom interrupted me. "What was Daddy like?" he said. "And there are enough people around that are going to say, 'Let me tell you what your daddy was like!' "

.   .   .

Minutes after the show ended, Hall, a former advertising executive who had, in midlife, dramatically altered his lifestyle and
his occupation, training to become a nurse, received a telephone call from his mother.

"John," she said. "I just watched *20/20*. Was that you I
saw?"

"Yes, Mother," Hall said.

"How did you ever get the part?" asked his mother.

Letters poured in to Tom from friends and strangers:

> My wife Karen, our children, my parents and my sisters send
> to you our deepest hopes and feelings.
>
> Your lifelong dedication to the ideals of being the best
> and your willingness to sacrifice to achieve goals that others
> only dream of have been an inspiration to me throughout my
> adult life. I greatly admire and respect you and consider my
> self uniquely fortunate to have been encouraged by you at a
> formative age. Many years have passed since the summer
> days at Camp To-Ho-Ne, but I remember so often how much
> you meant to all of us.
>
> Please feel our thoughts and prayers which are sent to
> you as you fight this great battle. I know you will be
> triumphant.
>
> Your friend,
> Jeffrey

> I've so many thoughts which I'd like to express, I hope you'll
> excuse any awkwardness.
>
> I'm sorry you're ill and that it took your sickness for me
> to reach out to you. Although we haven't stayed in touch, I

hear about you periodically and always think about all the good things you've done for so many people. . . .

Tom . . . I feel you've given a lot to me. Your honesty and willingness to take positions was a model for me and a constant reminder that we each have to march to our own drummer. You had the courage to be you and not be what Enge thought you should be, despite the hurt that caused both of you, I'm sure. And because you were so public a person and also a person I knew, it made it easier for me to step out of line, to find my drummer, to know someone I respected had already done so.

I don't mean to sound like I'm putting you on a pedestal, or that my roads were as daring as yours. I just want you to know that I admired you and hoped that in my life I would do as much for others as you have done.

I also want you to know that I've always thought of you as a friend, as part of my personal extended Enge family. . . .

I want to do something, somehow to make you better. I want to shout, "Hey, You up there. You can't do this to my friend Tom!" It might help if I believed there was a "You" to shout to, but I don't. . . .

I hope you don't mind my writing and I guess saying goodbye. I don't expect a reply. I just wanted to send my thoughts and some love.

Susan

I graduated from Springfield College in 1982 and am currently teaching and coaching in Massachusetts. I truly admire the honesty and openness with which you've lived your life. Watching the 20/20 piece, I remembered how strongly I guarded my closet while at SC, really living a double life as a leader on campus by day, and a regular at The Frontier, one of the two gay bars in Springfield, at night. I have imagined that we may have shared feelings of loneliness and isolation at SC, which I consider a wonderful school, albeit a bit homophobic. I'm sure that it was even worse in your time there.

My coming out process has been slow, and generally well supported. At about the time I was finally accepting my homosexuality, I was also beginning recovery from alcoholism in AA. . . . Tomorrow marks the third anniversary of my sobriety, and last week marked the second anniversary with my lover, whom I met in AA.

As I watched *20/20*, I felt a little more at ease about my upcoming reunion at Springfield. Your example has bolstered my sense of pride in my sexuality. While I am not ready to come out publicly, I do feel a lot more comfortable about sharing it with just the few people who already know.

Peace,
Mitch

You have shared your heart with the world, I hope the world can share her heart with you. . . . As a gay woman, I myself fervently hope to find a man willing to have a child with me. You have given me great hope for myself, and for the world. May God bless you and keep you, now and forever.

With much love,
Laura

On March 15th, I had the sad chance to know the tragedy of the virus when I lost the man I loved most in the world. Roy left us at the age of 32 and I'm still feeling it deeply. I lived with my lovable Mexican man for nearly eight years.

But I also wanted to point out something. . . . As an outreach of your first Gay Olympics, our French club is still going strong and every first Friday of the month, we still gather around, 40 men at a cocktail party in French, undoubtedly unique in the U.S. Also, I started about a year ago a similar social club for Spanish. Both successful and valuable groups are living monuments to the work and inspiration that Tom

Waddell spread all over Gay America and elsewhere. So many of us love you, care about you and are with you in our thoughts daily!

Love,
Armand

Men sent their love to Tom, and so did women—pure love from people who knew him and people who did not. Jan, his volunteer worker from the Shanti Project, a San Francisco organization that reached out to assist people with AIDS, sent him a copy of the first verse of W. H. Auden's "Lullaby," which Auden had written for a male lover.

Lay your sleeping head, my love,
Human on my faithless arm;
Time and fevers burn away
Individual beauty from
Thoughtful children, and the grave
Proves the child ephemeral:
But in my arms till break of day
Let the living creature lie,
Mortal, guilty, but to me
The entirely beautiful.

Tom also received more letters offering psychological and physical cures for AIDS—some of them guaranteed—and letters promising "total peace of mind" *if* "you turn your life over to the Lord." The latter missive ended: "If you have any questions about God, Christ, heaven or the Bible, please write to me."

Tom answered that letter, as he did almost every one.

In the spring and summer of 1987, the final seasons of his life, Tom divided his thoughts and energies between his child and his cause, between Jessica and the legal battle against the U.S. Olympic Committee. He laughed about the dresses that Jessica loved to wear, kidded Sara about how feminine their child was.

"There's a ninety percent chance she's going to be straight," Tom said. "Fine. Who cares? I don't care. And Sara doesn't care. It's whatever she is. The thing is, we want her to grow up feeling that she loves herself."

May 19, 1987

Since the last entry, I was getting so weak and lethargic I had to go to the hospital. They found my liver enlarged and some abnormal tests. I got a transfusion and went home, but didn't feel any better. A few days later, I was in the hospital again for some tests, and they discovered lymphoblastic lymphoma in my liver. It is a rather aggressive kind of cancer, and it was a real shocker because I had to stop the AZT treatment for the AIDS virus and start taking anti-cancer drugs (chemotherapy).

So my hair is falling out—with a little more help from you as you pull on it.

This was the final entry in Tom's journal for Jessica.

By the end of May 1987, six years after the Centers for Disease Control's first recorded case of "gay pneumonia," 36,058 American men, women, and children had been diagnosed with AIDS; and 20,849 had died. On May 31, 1987, President Reagan delivered his first speech on acquired immune deficiency syndrome.

On June 25, 1987, the Supreme Court of the United States ruled, by the narrowest possible margin—five justices to four—in favor of the United States Olympic Committee and against San Francisco Arts & Athletics Inc. and Thomas F. Waddell, M.D. The sanctity of the Olympic movement had been preserved; the Gay Games could not be called the Gay Olympics.

Tom was ready to die.

On the Fourth of July, Suellen Manning flew from Washington to San Francisco to help Eric Wilkinson nurse Tom through his final days. He explained to both of them that he wanted to hasten his end. He said he was glad that they could understand and accept his decision.

On July 7, Tom took himself off all medication—off the painkillers that blurred his memory, off the drugs that were supposed to slow or soften the ravages of AIDS. The next morning he went to the hospital and received three units of blood to give him a spurt of strength.

Then he went home and for the rest of the day, and deep into the following day, he and I sat and talked. He struggled for the memory to fill in the gaps in his life, to complete the frame of his autobiography. When he was satisfied that he had shared his story as well as he could, when he felt he could endure the frustrations of his failing mind no longer, he rested. He called Sara and Jessica to his bedside, handed his daughter the magic crystal ball, and kissed her goodbye.

Jessica had one final request. She wanted her mother and father to dance one last dance together. Sara helped Tom to his feet and supported him as they moved in a slow waltz. Of course, Sara led.

Early on Thursday evening, July 9, Tom told Eric that he wanted to hurry things along by taking morphine pills. Like many San Franciscans with AIDS, and with greater access than most, Tom had hoarded a supply of morphine. "They were small pills, a beautiful vivid purple," Eric recalled. "I brought a triangular dish of green tourmaline from the library outside Tom's bedroom and filled the green dish with purple pills. I took it in to Tom with a glass of water, and he smiled and said, 'How gay!'"

Eric and Suellen sat on the bed on each side of Tom, and my wife and I sat at the foot. Tom's feet were sticking out of the blankets. "I remember tucking the blankets around them for him," Eric said. "His big feet never fit comfortably in any bed and for the last few days of his life were always icy cold."

Eric helped Tom with the glass of water and the pills, which were difficult for him to swallow. After half an hour, he had managed to take thirty-six pills. "That should be enough," Dr. Waddell calculated. He winked at Eric and warned him that he was an accomplice.

It began to get dark outside, and no one spoke much. Eric and Suellen, both of whom had put in long hours caring for Tom, told him once more how much they loved him. He grew drowsier. His eyes flickered. And then he said, "Well, this should be interesting," and closed his eyes for the last time.

Eric and Suellen, and my wife and I sat quietly, watching Tom's breathing, gentle and even at first. Bill Strull left his own birthday party during the evening to look in on Tom and to reassure us that he was not suffering, that he was dying peacefully.

My wife and I kissed Tom goodbye and went back to our hotel room, preparing to leave San Francisco in the morning. Tom was deep in sleep but still breathing easily. Suellen was exhausted and lay down to rest in Jessica's room, next door to Tom's. Roger Tubb came up and kissed Tom goodbye. Eric pulled up a chair next to Tom's bed and fought exhaustion to stay awake through the night.

"Tom's breathing became quite stentorious," Eric said. "Every so often I would moisten a towel and wipe his forehead. He had been propped up on two pillows, but little by little he slipped down till his feet stuck out the bottom again. They were colder than ever as I tucked them up.

"In the middle of the night I woke with a start. Tom's breathing rhythm had changed. What looked to me like vomit had bubbled out of his nose and mouth and run down his cheek onto the blanket. I cleaned him up and tried to make him comfortable."

As Friday dawned, Suellen returned to Tom's side, and Eric went off to work at the Anchor Oyster Bay, a nearby restaurant. When Eric returned at 6 p.m., Tom was still alive, still unconscious, and a friend named Susan Shapiro had joined Suellen. The two of them and Eric sat with Tom through the evening. Late that night Eric was persuaded to go downstairs to sleep in his own bed.

At 7 a.m. on Saturday, July 11, 1987, Eric's phone rang. It was Suellen, asking him to come upstairs. Tom, she knew, was dying. Sara and Susan Shapiro were also summoned to Tom's side. "His breathing had become very uneven, very shallow," Eric said, "and as we held his hands, he died, quite peacefully."

Sara and Susan and Suellen and Eric cried and held one another. A few hours later, after Suellen and Susan laid out Tom's body, the funeral director from the corner of Albion and Seventeenth, only a block from Tom's house, arrived to take him away.

"I remember thinking that this was the last time he would ever come down those stairs and out that front door," Eric said.

The following morning, in the Sunday edition of the San Francisco *Examiner & Chronicle*, Bill Mandel, Tom's friend, wrote a love letter to Tom Waddell's daughter.

Dear Jessica:

You're not even 4 yet so this letter won't mean much to you now, but it's a letter I must write. I hope your mother keeps it for you to read when you get old enough.

Your father, Tom Waddell, the greatest man I have known, died Saturday morning, July 11, at 9 a.m. of acquired immune deficiency syndrome at 49. He died at home, peacefully, freed of the pain that had pummeled his proud body for more than a year.

Your mother, Sara Lewinstein, was with her husband when he died, as were a few of his dear friends. In a larger sense, your father's true friends—even those who'd never met him—were gathered about him in San Francisco and across the country. Today, we mourn.

Any child idolizes her father, but you, Jessica Waddell Lewinstein, have more reason than most kids. You spring from sterling stock. Your father was gifted with many talents, and he used them all to make his world—your world—a better place.

Tom was a healer. He was a physician, but that was just the beginning. His doctor's drive to cure extended far beyond ills of the body and applied itself to maladies of soul and culture.

I hope that when you get old enough to understand this note, there won't be small-minded bigots trying to shut the flow of love to any group of people. When your father was young, though, our society built walls to isolate people who were different from the majority.

Tom Waddell was a very strong man, strong enough to compete for the United States in the decathlon, the most challenging event, at the 1968 Olympic Games in Mexico City. A little later in his life, he used that strength to crash through the wall that prejudice built around homosexual people—people like your father and mother.

Your dad had everything. He could have kept his homosexuality a secret, but he decided that truth was a far greater goal than personal comfort . . .

Your father was a very brave man with an endless capacity for good works . . . he took on the challenge of organizing the "Gay Olympics . . ."

From hundreds of cities around the nation, they came to San Francisco, muscular with pride, happiness—and muscles. For generations, people like them had been forced to live shadowy, closeted lives. Now these athletes marched in a blaze of color around Kezar Stadium as thousands cheered and cried.

Thanks to your father and his allies in the fight for justice, a new era was dawning. Those Americans who cared to look through open eyes saw gay men and women as they really are . . .

You are a lucky girl in many ways, Jessica. You have grown up doubly enriched, doubly doted over by loving members of your parents' separate and overlapping worlds.

The joy of your birth coincided, sadly, with the arrival of the plague that would take your father's life. By the time of the 1986 Gay Games, the atmosphere in the gay community had changed drastically from the proud flag-waving days of 1982.

Tom was told he had AIDS as even larger throngs of athletes gathered in San Francisco last August for Gay Games II. Aware of the irony, your father tried to keep his diagnosis private, hoping the games would offer an antidote to the dread that was graying the community.

Already thin and pale, your dad marched arm-in-arm with your mother and other organizers of the games as thousands rose and cheered their progress across the green carpet of Kezar. Then Tom stood at the podium, trying to quiet the crowd that wouldn't let him speak for all its applause.

Knowing he faced death, he nevertheless told the audience and the world that the games showed the gay community as it was—strong, healthy, positive.

This was always his message: hope, optimism, love and struggle toward the light . . .

In the last weeks of his illness, your father was sad about

only one thing. He wanted so much to live to see you as an adult, to find out what kind of person you would become.

His dear friends told Tom they would stand in his stead to protect you and guide you. But there's little we can do to equal your father's greatest gift: his spirit, his tenacity, his love and his dedication. Through your veins flows the blood of two true champions, for your mother, Sara, is Tom's mate in heart and soul.

Sara called about two hours ago to say Tom had just died. Through her sadness and sense of loss, she said his life had been a victory. There is nothing I can add to that, but thanks that I was fortunate to know and be inspired by him.

It is a tragedy when a 3-year-old girl loses her father, even more so when her dad was so great a man. But in his lifetime your father created such a beacon of goodness in this world that its light will always illuminate your path.

Four days after Tom died, in the converted social and athletic hall in the Mission District of San Francisco, in the home that he had so painstakingly decorated, a couple of hundred of his friends gathered to tell stories about the man they loved, the man who was—in Zohn Artman's words—the role model for every homosexual in San Francisco. They came in business suits and in leather, and even in drag. A few of the Sisters of Perpetual Indulgence paraded outside the house.

At the celebration of Tom Waddell's life, a bearded, earnest man walked up to me and wondered if he could ask me a personal question. "Of course," I said.

"Have you ever undergone psychoanalysis?" he inquired.

"No," I said.

"That's funny," he said. "You're the first straight man I've met who seems at ease among homosexuals without psychoanalysis."

It was a compliment, I think.

• • •

A few days later, one week after Tom's death, more than four hundred people met in the rotunda at San Francisco City Hall to pay tribute to his achievements. "What he thought was good and right was what he devoted himself to," said Dr. David Werdegar, the director of the San Francisco Department of Health, which sponsored the tribute. "He had the courage of a great athlete, and he showed that that courage could be combined with humility."

Barry McDell, chairman of the Vancouver Athletics and Arts Association, which had been chosen to stage Gay Games III in 1990, called Tom an international hero to "thousands and thousands of gay men and women." McDell said Gay Games I "gave us the most significant gay or lesbian experience of our lives. Tom taught us not to fear being gay."

Mary Dunlap said her lasting vision of Tom would be as he appeared at the first Gay Games, "his tall, sleek, honest, brave form."

The crowd cheered each comment, but it cheered loudest when Sara Lewinstein announced that, the day before, the USOC had signed the official papers dropping the lien on the Albion Street house.

"I never thought I'd lose Tom this early," Sara told his admirers.

Many of the comments were not nearly so kind when my story, "The Death of an Athlete," appeared in the July 27, 1987, issue of *Sports Illustrated*:

> "Although I'm only 17, I have subscribed to *Sports Illustrated* for seven years, and I have never read a more nauseating article than 'The Death of an Athlete.'"

"These QUEERS, these inhuman excuses for real people, are an abomination to the human race—yet you trash up what was a fine magazine with a feature article about one. Totally disgusting."

"Dick Schaap's article on homosexual Tom Waddell should never have been printed in your usually excellent sports magazine. A man who commits the immoral and unnatural act of being gay should not be idolized after God judges him for his actions."

"I was shocked and disgusted to read about Waddell's fathering of a daughter with a lesbian."

"God has already begun to judge our nation because of the likes of the person in your article. Let us hope the process is not irreversible. Tom Waddell was not a man of Olympian spirit, but rather a man of perverse spirit who paid with his life for that which God and man alike call an abomination. The homosexual lifestyle does not deserve sympathy, but rather condemnation."

"The worst and most disgusting story ever published in *Sports Illustrated*. . . . His death was simply a side effect of the loathsome lifestyle he went about promoting."

"Faggots and lesbians are the disease! That faggot farm he went to scares me to death! Faggots producing more faggots and you print the trash!"

"Cancel my subscription."

"We will never resubscribe to *SI* again."

Clearly, Tom Waddell's crusade against prejudice and ignorance still had many miles to go. But not all of the letters were
negative. At least half of them applauded both the magazine
and the article.

"I am sure you will receive many rude letters and calls
from homophobic jerks . . . but if just one person's
attitude regarding AIDS and the gay population is
changed, Waddell's life was not lost in vain.

"I am not a homosexual, an athlete or a doctor, but
Tom Waddell's courage and fortitude will always serve
as an inspiration to me. Again, thank you for an important article which is indicative of the reasons I continue
to subscribe to *Sports Illustrated*."

"Dr. Waddell was a terrific person who also happened to be gay. The two are not mutually exclusive,
and never have been."

"Never in my life have I been so moved by a magazine article. I publish a magazine and at the last staff
meeting gave out copies of the article along with these
words, 'Ladies and gentlemen, this is what magazine
journalism is all about. . . .'

"Thank you for adding considerably to the quality
of my life."

"Your piece on Tom Waddell was the most inspired
and inspiring piece I've read in such a long time that
I'm hard pressed to find its equal. I just read it minutes
ago, and as I write, the tears keep re-forming as I remember what you wrote and what he lived. As you
said, he was quite a man; as you are—for sharing his
story in such a generous and gifted Olympian spirit."

"It's the most powerful and moving article I've ever read in *SI*—and I go all the way back to the first issue and still have it in my files."

A few months after Tom died, a group of Springfield College students, coaches, teachers, and alumni gathered at the school's Marsh Memorial Hall to remember a distinguished graduate. Jack Savoia, who had been Tom's teammate in track and field, spoke; so did Sara Lewinstein. During Sara's remarks, Jessica sneaked up on the stage behind her and put her head under her mother's skirt. "I didn't teach her that," Sara said. "Honest, I didn't." And both Sara and her audience laughed.

Ironically, when Tom's death was reported in a Springfield publication, there was no mention of his homosexuality or of AIDS. The publication carefully enumerated Tom's athletic achievements and pointedly mentioned his wife and his daughter, but did not allude to the Gay Games. Jack Savoia was among the Springfield alumni who met with the college's president to protest the "sanitizing" of Tom's life.

Zohn Artman died a few months after Tom. Charles Deaton died, too. Deaton had visited Tom during the final year of his life, had reminisced and had said goodbye. He, too, was very sick at the time. Eric Wilkinson tried to contact Charles after Tom's death but was unable to find him.

At the time of Tom's death, the city of San Francisco had begun to mount a serious bid to host the 1996 Olympic Games. Gay activists, spurred by the U.S. Olympic Committee's opposition to the Gay Olympics, lobbied to keep the Games away.

Partly because of the gay opposition to San Francisco, and

largely because of the influence of the Coca-Cola Company, Atlanta was awarded the 1996 Olympics. Sara Lewinstein was among those who felt that the gay community's anti-Olympic protests were misconceived and misdirected. "The perception has been created that somehow gays hate the Olympics," Sara told the *Chronicle*. "That's crazy. We love the Olympics. We just don't like the dumb bureaucrats who run the USOC. I think Tom would have loved having the Olympics here. For one thing, there would have been better sports facilities built all over the city. Tom always wanted an Olympic-size pool in San Francisco."

Bill Mandel, too, felt that Tom's memory was being misused. "We shape their memories into convenient symbols, and then bronze what we've built," Mandel said of Tom Waddell, Harvey Milk, and other heroes. "It's odd to see people we've known personally deprived by history of their human-scale fullness as they're turned into larger-than-life two-dimensional icons, the better to fit on demonstrators' placards. . . . It's possible, after all, that Joan of Arc talked with her mouth full.

"Comparing the real Waddell I knew with the martyr Waddell who's emerging a year after his death, I fear I'm losing the real 3-D Tom, the Tom with the wicked sense of humor, obsessive desire for neatness and continual taste for the sensual.

"Perhaps it's the fate of martyrs never to be free of suffering, even after death."

In 1988, the San Francisco Central Aid Station was renamed the Tom Waddell Clinic, and "Threads of Love," the Names Project quilt, was displayed not far away at the Moscone Center. "Inspired by the American folk art traditions of quilting and sewing bees," said the program for the display, "the Names Project is a nationwide campaign to memorialize the tens of thousands of Americans who have been killed by the AIDS epidemic. The Names Project quilt is composed of thousands of fabric panels, each bearing the name of an individual who has died of AIDS. Designed and completed in homes across America by the friends, lovers and families of those memorialized, the panels are stitched together by volunteers into the ever-growing quilt."

By the end of 1988, the quilt was composed of 8,738 panels. Some people were memorialized in more than one panel. There were four panels bearing the name of Rock Hudson. There were three remembering Zohn Artman. Only one individual was represented by seven panels: Tom Waddell.

Gay Games III was held in Vancouver in 1990, and more than 7,000 athletes competed. The setting was beautiful; the city embraced its guests. And the mistress of ceremonies at the opening ceremonies, a lesbian comedienne, explained that being a lesbian was a state of mind, not a physical thing. "For instance," she said, "if I never have sex with another woman for the rest of my life, I will still be a lesbian." She paused, and then added, "But not a happy lesbian."

Tom would have relished the laughter.

In 1994, Gay Games IV came to New York City, coincidental with the twenty-fifth anniversary of Stonewall, the historic Greenwich Village confrontation between the gay community and the police. Martina Navratilova, perhaps the greatest woman tennis player who ever lived, and a lesbian, offered fund-raising support. Greg Louganis, the great diver, and a gay man, offered vocal support. "I'm real excited to be part of an event that's all about the true Olympic ideals," Louganis said. "This is our chance to show ourselves and the world how strong we are as individuals and as a community."

Louganis, who had long kept his sexual orientation private, greeted the Gay Olympians with the declaration, "It's great to be out and proud."

The fourth edition of Tom Waddell's dream attracted 10,879 athletes, making it the largest multisport athletic field in history, exceeding even the 1992 Olympic Games in Barcelona. The closing ceremonies jammed Yankee Stadium with more than 50,000 people. Participants ranged in skill from Bruce Hayes, a swimmer who had earned a gold medal in the 1984 Olympic Games in Los Angeles; to Sara Lewinstein, who, despite a lack of practice and competition, bowled a sensational 265 game; to me.

I entered the tennis competition, paired in men's over-55 doubles with Tom's friend and Roger Tubbs's employer, Jim Hormel, a generous backer of the Gay Games. We won a bronze medal, but not because of any great prowess on our part. Only eight teams were entered in our division, and when our opponents failed to appear for the quarter-final match— I presume they were intimidated—we advanced by default to the semis. There we were soundly beaten, but, like the other unsuccessful semifinal team, were awarded third-place medals.

During the match which ended our participation, I demonstrated the one skill that separates my game from other, equally mediocre efforts: I hit forehands with either hand. The first time I swatted a left-handed forehand for a winner, one of our opponents stopped, did a double take and called to me, "Are you bi-?"

I couldn't resist. "I thought you'd never ask," I said.

The coverage of the Gay Games was remarkable; more than fifty articles appeared in the New York *Times* alone. Anna Quindlen, the columnist, wrote:

> The Games, which have been going on at pools, skating rinks and gymnasiums throughout the area, are a terrible

threat to those who believe that America's house needs more closets. Because as men and women in warm-up clothes have stepped onto subway trains, gay cops have helped out with security and gay athletes have challenged world records, the Games have come to illustrate the myriad ways in which gay men and lesbians are now part of the mainstream. . . .

They're here. They're queer. They're on television, talking about their moms, their kids and their lovers. The other night Geraldo led a discussion of the issues. His guests included gay activist-athletes and a straight opponent who runs one of those organizations that's supposed to stand for family values. The gay guests were calm and courteous. The family man was obnoxious and rude, the sort of person who gives heteros a bad name. It was no contest in the humanity event. . . .

. . . watching all these proud competitors gathered beneath their own multicolored flag, the risk was very real of seeing them as they really are. And that would be the most dangerous thing that could ever happen to the homophobes. Bottom line, it puts them out of business.

On its editorial page, the *Times* commented on the Games:

June has been an enlightening, and enlightened, month in New York City. Gotham's citizens could hardly turn on their television sets or ride the subways without encountering some aspect of the astoundingly large gay presence that had converged on the city.

Gay Games IV brought 11,000 athletes and tens of thousands of sports fans from 40 countries. More than 130 cultural events celebrated gay themes. And on Sunday, tens of thousands of gay men and lesbians marched to commemorate the evening in 1969 when police, harassing patrons of a gay Greenwich Village bar called the Stonewall Inn, met fierce resistance for the first time.

The gay rights struggle has often been likened to the struggle of blacks or women for equality. But there was one crucial difference. It was nearly always clear when a black person or a woman had entered the room. Gay Americans, by contrast, have lived largely as an indistinguishable minority. Bigots insulted them to their faces without knowing it, and were often unaware of just how many gay people there were. And homosexuals whose orientation became known were easily isolated as "abnormal."

Stonewall taught that while invisible people had no rights, gay people who stood together had a far better chance of achieving recognition. The growing gay components in both the Democratic and Republican Parties provide ample evidence today that the lessons of Stonewall have been taken to heart. So did the recent celebrations in New York.

Police estimated the final crowd in Central Park at 100,000, although organizers insist it was far larger. Along the main parade route, marchers unfurled a 20-block-long rainbow-colored flag. They were a splendidly diverse multitude: Democrats and Republicans; moderates, radicals and conservatives; drag queens in glittering gowns; a Marine lance corporal in dress uniform; a former FBI agent; a police officer; an Eskimo from Alaska.

Many participants found the experience profoundly liberating, a mass statement that their movement had arrived and could never be shoved back into the closet. As one organizer said: "We will never turn back. We will never be invisible again."

Tom would have been proud of many things at Gay Games IV, but most of all, of his daughter. Jessica Waddell Lewin-

stein, who was about to turn eleven, was an important part of
the opening ceremonies at Columbia University's Wien Stadium. She stood in front of thousands of people her father had
brought together and read a poem she had written. The poem
was called "I Remember":

> I remember when I had my 1st, 2nd & 3rd birthday.
> I remember when I cut out my paper dolls in half.
> I remember when I would play the piano & would hear
>   my dad clap in the other room.
> I remember the time when I last saw my dad.
> I remember the time when I fell off the stage on Christmas.
> I remember the good times we had.
> I remember the way he acted to make me happy.
> I remember all these things and more just because of me
>   and my brain.
> I remember when my dad would come home from work
>   and say hello to the family.
> I remember when my dad came to pick me up from
>   Montessori and all the kids would say how lucky I am
>   to have a father like mine & then they would run to
>   him and say "take off your thumb" so he did and I felt
>   wonderful. It was just a trick though, but I never knew
>   that.
> I remember my dad and everything else.
> I remember my teacher Mr. Jon Dorus who had the same
>   thing happen to him as my dad. And I loved him
>   because I knew him all my life.

I wish Tom could have seen her.

Acknowledgments

First I want to thank all those unsuspecting people who have sat next to me on airplanes in recent years, whom I conned into reading the first twenty or thirty or forty pages of the Tom Waddell manuscript, almost all of whom seemed to be gripped by Tom's story and urged me to overcome the block that had drastically slowed down my writing. They were kind enough to say they very much wanted to read the rest of the book.

The block was Tom's fault. If he hadn't been such an incredible human being, if I hadn't felt such pressure to produce a manuscript that measured up to his standards, and if he hadn't died, if he hadn't left me without my most valuable source, the best witness to corroborate facts and theories and anecdotes, I suspect I would have completed this book in less than eight years.

It probably would have taken me even longer, however, without the help of many kind and supportive people, most notably David Levine, who put much of my research into cohesive order, who pointed and prodded me in the right direction, and Eric Wilkinson, Tom's friend and tenant. When I desperately needed Eric's guidance, he flew from San Francisco to New York, literally moved into my office, and for ten days sat by my side as I wrote, answering my questions and filling in the gaps as well as he could, which was as well as anyone could. I might never have completed the book without the aid of David and Eric.

I want to thank Sara Lewinstein for doing what so many Jewish women, starting with my mother, have done for me during my lifetime—laying guilt on me. Sara, sometimes gently, sometimes firmly, made me feel as if I were committing a heinous act if I were not at work on the manuscript. My wife, Trish, laid gentle guilt on me, which can also be compelling, and she read every page faithfully and repeatedly, in manuscript and in galleys, always cheering me on.

Jay Hill was an enormous help. I met Jay when he was working at the Winter Olympic Games in Calgary in 1986 as a researcher for ABC Sports. I knew he was a good researcher. I asked him to help me with this story, never suspecting what I was getting him into. Jay ended up as executive director of Gay Games IV, the spectacular New York festival of 1994.

I thank Zohn Artman, who shared his love for Tom with me, his great store of stories and opinions, and his zest for good food. Because of his position with Bill Graham, Zohn could even help me get tickets for Grateful Dead concerts. My access to those tickets may be the only way I've ever impressed one of my daughters, Joanna, who put in a tour as a Deadhead. One of my sons, Jeremy, conducted several interviews at Springfield College.

So many of Tom's friends were helpful, from Jack Savoia, his college teammate, to Steve Schwartz, his army buddy, to Jim Hormel, his Dunies buddy. Roger Tubb was always kind to me; so was Suellen Manning. Marjorie Margolies-Medvinsky, with whom I once worked, generously shared her memories, and so did another woman who loved Tom, Taffy Van Dyke Bruce. Jackie Leonard, one of Tom's mentors at The Farm, was kind enough to read parts of the manuscript and to suggest emendations.

A pair of writers, Paul Moor and Mark Messner, shared with me interviews they had conducted with Tom Waddell. Messner is a professor of psychology and a former athlete, co-author of *Sex, Violence and Power in Sports*. A young man named Andrew Leone helped in the early stages of the research, and the columns of Bill Mandel were an inspiration.

My editor, Ash Green, was heroically patient, and, as always, equally perceptive. His assistant, Jennifer Bernstein, was the perfect liaison, and a pair of literary agents, Sterling Lord, who represented me for decades, and David Black, who represents me now, offered excellent advice and counsel.

I apologize to those I've overlooked, but I do want to thank everyone who made me feel at home in the gay community of San Francisco. I was so comfortable that one night, when Sara dropped me at her restaurant, Artemis, I was in there for several minutes before I realized that, among perhaps one hundred patrons, I was the only male in the place.

The next day I described the scene to my wife, who asked me, "Were they all gay?"

"I don't know," I said. "I suppose so."

"You know," she said, "that's the trouble with your fantasies. They always have a hitch in them."

Tom would have laughed, too. Thanks, Tom.

A NOTE ABOUT THE AUTHORS

Tom Waddell always wanted to write a book, but thought life would give him more time to do it. During his forty-nine years, he excelled at athletics, at medicine, and at living. He won countless medals and even more friends. He was married to Sara Lewinstein and was the father of Jessica Waddell Lewinstein.

Dick Schaap is a correspondent for ABC News, host of ESPN's "The Sports Reporters," and sports editor of *Parade* magazine. His televised profiles and features have reaped five Emmy Awards, and his coverage of every Olympics since 1976 has won him widespread critical praise. A collegiate lacrosse player, he is a member of the Cornell Athletic Hall of Fame. He has collaborated on best-selling autobiographies with Bo Jackson, Jerry Kramer, and Joe Montana. *Gay Olympian* is his thirtieth book. He lives in Manhattan with his wife, Trish, and their children, Kari and David.

A NOTE ON THE TYPE

This book was set in Caledonia, a Linotype face designed by W. A. Dwiggins (1880–1956). It belongs to the family of printing types called "modern face" by printers—a term used to mark the change in style of the type letters that occurred around 1800. Caledonia borders on the general design of Scotch Roman but it's more freely drawn than that letter.

Composed by Creative Graphics, Allentown, Pennsylvania
Printed and bound by Quebecor Printing Martinsburg, Martinsburg, West Virginia
Designed by Robert C. Olsson